# Solidar

C000071943

## on the

# Waterfront:

### *The Liverpool Lock Out of 1995/96*

*by*

*Michael Lavalette and Jane Kennedy*

*Front cover:*
*Dockers' Demonstration, Pier Head, Liverpool, 28 September 1996.*
*Mersey Docks and Harbour Building in the background.*

First published 1996 by Liver Press, 1 & 3 Grove Road, Rock Ferry, Birkenhead, Wirral, Merseyside L42 3XS.

British Library Cataloguing in Publication Data.
A catalogue record for this book is available from the British Library.
ISBN 1 871201 06 3

*It may seem over indulgent but I would like to take this opportunity to dedicate this book to my daughter Olivia, in the hope that the struggle of the Liverpool dockers and their families will enable her to live (and eventually work) in a better world and certainly one where casualisation has been abolished for ever.*

Michael Lavalette
October 1996


*I would like to dedicate this book to my mum and to the memory of my dad, and to thank them for always believing that I could achieve what I wanted*

Jane Kennedy
October 1996

# Acknowledgements

This booklet could not have been written without the active help and support of many people. We would like to take this opportunity to thank them. First, and foremost, to the dockers and their families who were and are an inspiration to us all. For over twelve months they have fought against the odds with strength, initiative, determination and humour. Second, more particularly, to those who spent hours talking to us and offered us a very personal record of the Liverpool lock-out. Third, the stewards have been very free with their time when they have had better and more important things to do. From an organisational perspective Geoff Jones, Billy Jenkins and Bob Ritchie organised many of the interviews and made our lives a lot easier. A number of people have read and commented on the script. Their advice has often been contradictory but it has been helpful to us nevertheless. In particular thanks to Laura Penketh, Pete Marsden, Rita Gough, Chris Jones, Tony Novak, Tony Lane and Julie Waterson. The readers from Liver Press were Eric Taplin and Sam Davies and both subjected the text and our ideas to considerable criticism and forced us to think about some of our arguments. Responsibility for what appears here, of course, rests with us.

Michael Lavalette
Jane Kennedy
October 1996

# Contents

# Foreword

The lock-out of the Liverpool dockworkers in 1995 and 1996 led to one of the most heroic strikes in the recent history of the British labour movement. As employers all over the country, encouraged by a reactionary and corrupt government, broke up unions, cut wages, sped up machines and increased worker-harassment, the reaction of the labour leaders was to shrug their shoulders and cringe before the onslaught. The Liverpool dockers and their families refused to cringe. They set up a ferocious and stubborn resistance which shook employers to their roots. At one stage, when the dockers turned down a huge bribe to call off their strike, tens of millions of pounds was wiped off the stock market value of the Mersey Docks and Harbour company.

As this book graphically describes in its first few pages, the strike was "manufactured". The Liverpool dock employers had watched their counterparts all over the country cash in on the Tory government's 1989 law which smashed the cherished dock labour scheme, and plunged the industry back into the dark days of casualised labour, and reduced wages and conditions of dockers over the country. In Hull, London, Bristol, Southampton and the other great ports, trade unionist dockers had been sacked wholesale, usually illegally, and replaced by non-union or docile labour which worked harder for less money. The chief result was enormous riches for a handful of third-rate employers. Employers on the Mersey didn't see why they should put up any longer with a unionised workforce which insisted on decent standards for its workers. The strike was therefore engineered so that all the dockers could be sacked and the trade union broken.

The resistance was entirely unexpected. The best part of this book tells of the experience of the strikers as they travelled the country and the world in search of support and of the growth of Women on the Waterfront, an entirely new organisation formed by dockers' wives, daughters and sisters. I record here that after one of the great dockers' rallies in Liverpool two friends from Canada who had been there came to stay in my house. They had some experience in the Labour movement on both sides of the Atlantic but declared at once that the speech made by Doreen McNally, one of the founders of WOW, was by a long way the best they had ever heard in their lives. Warm, passionate, furious, funny: all the best characteristics of the working people of Liverpool rolled into one glorious onslaught.

An extraordinary feature of the dispute which is clearly set out here is that the dockers got overwhelming support everywhere they went - except in the offices of their own trade union. The leaders of one of the biggest and most powerful unions on earth sat back and watched the cream of their membership struggle alone. The leaders' excuse was that they were bound by the Tories' anti-union laws, under which, technically, the strike was "secondary action". But the excuse was really a cover for the union leaders' own craven pusillanimity. This pusillanimity had grown with years of connivance with laws which were made to break their organisations. The reply of the union general secretary to the appeal from Women on the Waterfront, which is set out in this book, was the nadir of this pusillanimity.

Reading this book in mounting anger and disgust, my mind kept turning back to the directors of the Mersey Docks and Harbour, a big company in which the government has a large stake.

All of these men imagine themselves to be pillars of the community, doyens of the Chamber of Commerce, who came to their aid so often, members of the Rotary Club and the Round Table, almost certainly officials at their church. How was it that they came to behave like wild animals to their fellow human beings who were working with them in the same enterprise? How could they plot so cruelly to destroy the jobs and livelihoods of so many people who, as their own publications confirmed, were some of the most hard-working and competent dockers in the world? The answer comes from a single word: exploitation. There can be no other explanation for this shocking story but that the world is divided into haves and have-nots, and that the haves work single-mindedly night and day to boost their wealth and power at the expense of the have-nots. Michael Lavalette and Jane Kennedy's marvellous account of a marvellous resistance never once loses its indignation at the behaviour of the employers and the support they received for their barbaric behaviour from other barbarians in their class. Every trade unionist in the country should read it.

*Paul Foot*

*November 1996*

# Chronology of Events

**June 1989**      Abolition of the National Dock Labour Scheme (NDLS), Re-organsation of MDHC operation into six separate areas,

**Jan 1991**      Formation of Torside Ltd

**May 1991**      Initial Recruitment of 30 Torside employees

**Nov 1991**      Second intake of 30 Torside employees

**July 1992**      Derecognition of all 12 elected TGWU shop stewards

**Aug 1992**      Third intake of 20 Torside employees

**March 1994**      New Contracts Imposed on MDHC dockers

**July 1995**      20 redundancies announced by Torside

**Aug 1995**      Official ballot by Torside employees votes in favour of strike action.

**Sept 1995**      Redundancies called off by Torside

**25 Sept 1995**      Torside employees ordered to break negotiated agreement and work a ship at short notice and without normal overtime arrangements; 5 Torside workers sacked.

**26 Sept 1995**      80 Torside dockers sacked

**28 Sept 1995**      Pickets setup by Torside workers at entrance to Seaforth Container Terminal

**29 Sept 1995**      MDHC claim dockers have sacked themselves

**29-30 Sept 1995**      New contracts issued to approximately 200 dockers

**6 Oct 1995**      P45's issued by MDHC

**9 & 10 Oct 1995**      Following advice from TGWU, MDHC dockers vote to return to work but are locked out by MDHC

**18 Oct 1995**      First 'Final offer'

**21 Oct 1995**      First community demonstration in support of the dockers

**Nov & Dec 1995**      Series of mass pickets attracting workers from throughout the country.

**15-21 Dec 1995**      Liverpool pickets stop work in US docks, as a consquence ACL give MDHC ultimatum: 'settle the dispute or we pull out of Liverpool',

**25 Jan 1996**      Second 'Final offer'

**8 Feb 1996**      Ballot overwhelmingly rejects MDHC offer

**19 Feb-**

**23 Feb 1996**      International conference held at Liverpool Town Hall

| | |
|---|---|
| **27 April 1996** | First national support group conference held in Liverpool, resolution passed formerly set-up national support group network. |
| **1 May 1996** | Merseyide Day of Action in support of dockers, rally in city centre addressed by Paul Foot. |
| **4 May 1996** | Second national support group conference, |
| **4 June 1996** | Third 'Final offer' presented by MDHC at meeting with ACAS |
| **7 June 1996** | Third offer unanimously rejected at dockers' mass meeting. |
| **21 June 1996** | ACL pull out of the port |
| **July 1996** | 4 Liverpool dockers occupy port in Quebec to attract attention to CAST's continuing use of Liverpool Port. |
| **20 July 1996** | Third national support group conference (first held on delegate basis) |
| **23 July 1996** | ACL announce return to Liverpool from 24 July |
| **31 Aug/1 Sept 1996** | Second International Conference |
| **9 Sept 1996** | Lobby of TUC Conference (Blackpool) |
| **28 Sept 1996** | First Anniversary March and Rally |
| **30 Sept 1996** | International Day of Action |

# Introduction

On the 25 September 1995, 22 workers employed by the Torside docks company in Liverpool were informed by managers that they would have to work overtime to get a ship ready for sailing. Although the notice was short (20 minutes before the end of the shift) the dockers had become increasingly used to such demands. What they were not used to was the news that 'normal overtime arrangements' would not apply. The short notice and the payment arrangements both breached existing agreements between Mersey Docks and Harbour Company (MDHC), Torside Ltd and the Transport and General Workers Union (TGWU). Taken aback, the dockers decided to discuss the situation with their shop stewards, who had been instructed that day to work at another dock within the Merseyside complex. As the working day finished, the men left the ship and went to the canteen to wait for the stewards. As the first group of five dockers arrived they were met by the Managing Director of the Torside company, who sacked them for leaving the ship. Bewildered, they wandered out to meet the others and tell them what had happened. When they in turn went into the canteen they were informed that they should go back to the ship, without their five sacked colleagues, or they would suffer the same fate; they refused to go back on such terms and were sacked.

The next morning (26 September) the remainder of the Torside workforce gradually heard what had happened and a quick meeting with the stewards was arranged for 8 a.m.. Over the previous evening the MDHC Port Stewards had advised the Torside stewards and workforce to go to work and let the senior stewards and the TGWU Docks Officer (Jack Dempsey) deal with the sackings via negotiation and the 'normal' grievance procedures. However, the situation was further inflamed by the Managing Director of Torside Ltd who appeared at the canteen meeting and sacked the entire workforce. On the morning of the 27 September the Torside workforce mounted a picket of the Nelson Freight Company (a part-owned

1

subsidiary of MDHC). The Torside men regularly worked side by side with dockers from Nelson Freight and the dockers (11 in all) refused to cross the picket line. As a consequence they were sacked by MDHC.

Despite this the MDHC Port Stewards still advocated a return to work. The main workforce were now in the Royal Seaforth docks (the main sector of the Merseyside docks complex) giving the stewards and the TGWU official a further day to resolve to dispute. The official, however, was 'not available', Torside claimed to have gone into voluntary liquidation (though twelve months into the dispute they remain listed as a going concern at Companies House) and MDHC refused to discuss the issue because they claimed it was an internal dispute at an independent company. Frustrated and angry, the sacked workers decided to leaflet the Seaforth docks informing the men there of their plight and notifying them a picket would be in place on the morning of the 28 September. The local union official, though 'not available', was able to refuse the Torside workers facilities to produce their leaflets. However, the local unemployed centre provided use of a photocopier and the workforce paid for their leaflets to be produced. On the morning of the 28th the pickets were in place and the Seaforth workforce refused to cross the lines. In response the entire workforce was sacked by MDHC: in the space of 4 days almost 500 workers had lost their jobs and been locked out of work. MDHC proceeded to enter a contract with Drake International, a London-based employment agency, to provide casual labour in the docks complex. Over the next few days they recruited their workforce from throughout Britain and housed them on the docks: Liverpool had become a 'Scab Port'.

The Liverpool dispute is important for four inter-related reasons. First, the events of September 1995 were the continuation of a strategy of casualisation that had been put in place in the wake of the abolition of the National Dock Labour Scheme (NDLS) in June 1989 and the conditions on the docks in the run up to the dispute emphasise the 'social costs of casualisation'. Unregulated, casualised employment not only detrimentally impacts on the workers directly involved, but it spreads beyond the workplace, affecting families, family relations and social life.

Second, the evidence makes it clear that the dispute was clearly manufactured. It was part of a conscious management strategy to weaken the union, isolate rank and file militants and casualise the dock workforce. Interestingly on the BBC television programme *Close Up North* (29/2/96) an unnamed and unidentified scab justified his refusal to join the dispute because he knew that it had been manufactured by MDHC to rid the docks of "militants who they knew would not cross a picket line". In the same programme Bernard Cliffe, managing director of MDHC, questioned the abilities and fitness of the sacked dockers alleging that, because of their age, they were unable to adapt to new machinery and worked too slowly. However, such claims contrast sharply with a report in Lloyds List (15/9/95), two weeks before the dispute, that described the Liverpool workforce as "the best in Europe" and made no reference to problems caused by age or lack of skills. The aggressive 'macho' management style adopted by MDHC is normally associated with the worst industrial relations practices in the USA or the Newly Industrialising Countries, or is perhaps assumed to be a relic of our industrial past, but the reality is that these tactics are increasingly common within Britain and have developed over the last 17 years in a government-fostered atmosphere of anti-unionism.[1] As an editorial in Lloyds List claimed:

> mass sackings, with the employers acting in a muscular fashion, is a reminder of a bad old past.[2]

The consequences of such practices, however, are not merely 'industrial': 500 dockers and their families face poverty and ruin as a result.

The third point is that the tactics of MDHC have not gone unchallenged. Although locked out, the 500 dockers and their families have refused to accept management's 'right to manage' in such a callous way and have mounted a significant challenge to both MDHC and the government, who are backing them and have created and encouraged the conditions for such a managerial style to develop. At the time of writing (September 1996) the dockers have been locked-out for twelve months. Throughout this time there have been daily pickets on the dock gates with cargo throughput reduced as a result, prompting MDHC to take out substantial advertising space in the local press warning of the economic effects of the dispute.[3] Delegates have been sent throughout Britain and the world to look for financial, moral and practical support for the dockers' cause. As a result, there has been a number of mass pickets and demonstrations in Liverpool, actions taken against companies using the Port and international disruption of shipping lines using Liverpool docks. An international dockers' conference was held in Liverpool from 18 to 23 February 1996 and produced a resolution from delegates promising significant international disruption of ships using the Liverpool docks. 'Women of the Waterfront' (WOW), the women's support group, have picketed the houses of scabs and managers, and have themselves been abroad to rally support. Dockers support groups have been set up throughout the country in a way that has not been seen since the Miners' Strike of 1984/85. The dispute emphasises the fact that trade unionism, the 'dinosaur' of New Labour-speak, is alive and fighting in Britain and that it remains the most powerful opponent of government social and economic policy. Further, as the story unfolds, it is clear that the struggle itself has a dynamic of its own and changes peoples' views and outlook on life. At the start of the dispute the dockers and their families were fatigued and demoralised as a consequence of the increasing job casualisation, 'flexible' work arrangements, increasing hours and the decline in take home pay. After twelve months in dispute the dockers and their families have changed: they travel the country and the world addressing mass meetings and their self-belief in their own abilities to change and shape the world has grown immeasurably.

Finally, the dispute poses questions about the role of the leadership of the labour and trade union movement. For twelve months the TGWU has refused to make the dispute official and the Labour Party has done everything within its power to dissociate itself from it (unlike the Conservative Party which was not slow to rally to the support of MDHC). The prospect of the Labour Party winning the next election means that workers are under huge pressure not to rock the boat but to wait for a Labour government. However, such a prognosis does not help those workers facing redundancy and hardship now, several months before the General Election. Further, Labour's actions increasingly brings the issue of 'what type of government Labour will be' into sharp focus. 'New Labour' is desperately trying to show potential middle class voters that it is qualitatively and quantitatively different from 'Old Labour', perceived as being tied to the 'union barons'. This means abandoning Labour's traditional supporters, turning away from issues of 'work', unemployment and poverty and raising the possibility of formerly breaking its historic link with the trade union movement.[4] Instead Labour now focuses on policies constructed around Thatcherite themes of 'sound money', cuts in public spending and low taxation.

In these circumstances the leadership of the unions and the TUC are under huge pressure not to threaten electoral success, and any form of industrial action is seen as potentially disastrous to Labour's electoral chances. Throughout the summer of 1996 high profile disputes on London Underground and in the Post Office brought the direct intervention of the Labour Party leadership, arguing against strikes that were against the 'public interest' and raising the possibility of a new Labour Government introducing new Industrial Relations Laws to further restrict trade union activities and the right to strike. In Liverpool, a more localised dispute, the Labour leadership has had little to say, but has clearly fostered an atmosphere that discourages any form of high profile, or officially backed, secondary action. The consequence for the Liverpool dockers is that they have been left to fight using their own resources. The Liverpool dock workers have shown, and continue to show, great resilience, strength and determination. They run the dispute from the weekly mass meetings where all decisions are debated and voted on. They have received substantial solidarity from workers throughout Britain and from dockers, longshoremen and 'wharfies' across the globe. Yet, there are parts of Britain where the twelve month struggle is unheard of and there are even TGWU branches who still claim no knowledge of the dispute, despite a pledge by Bill Morris and Jack Adams from the TGWU leadership that they would actively publicise the dispute to union branches. Official backing would bring national recognition, aid the spread of further solidarity and raise the possibility of substantial secondary action in Britain which, along with the growing international boycott, could create the conditions for a magnificent return to work: a just victory for the Liverpool dockers and one whose ramifications would spread far beyond Merseyside.

This book aims to look at these issues. It is primarily based on a number of interviews conducted by the authors with dockers and their families, supplemented, where appropriate, by relevant secondary sources. Wherever possible, we let the participants tell the story in their own words. This is after all the story of 500 dock families fighting for jobs and the consequences and changes brought about by their struggle. Chapter 1 offers a recent history of dock work and culture and argues that this history is important because it shapes many of the values and commitments of the dockers locked in dispute with MDHC. Chapter 2, more immediately, looks at changes that have occurred on the docks since the abolition of the National Dock Labour Scheme (NDLS) in 1989. These changes have had a significant and deleterious effect on the dockers, their working, home and social lives and, by implication therefore, have also been experienced by both dock families and dock communities. It is both the 'breadth' and extent of the social costs of recent casualisation of dock work that accounts for the strength and determination of the dockers and their families in the present dispute. Chapter 3 looks at Women of the Waterfront, the women's support group who have played an increasingly active role in the dispute. The women of WOW are the clearest example of a group whose lives have been changed dramatically by the events of the last twelve months and this chapter explores this issue in some detail. Chapter 4 focuses on the major events of the last year and provides a chronological account of the dispute to date. Chapters 5 and 6 look at the extent and form of solidarity received by the dockers. Chapter 5 looks at the situation in Britain while Chapter 6 looks at international solidarity. We conclude by looking to the future: MDHC's plans for the docks and their consequences for the people and environment of Liverpool; and the prospect for a dockers' victory which may shift the balance away from MDHC's ruthless profit maximisation drive and in favour of better jobs and conditions of work, for more full time dockers, in the Mersey docks complex.

Finally, to emphasise that this is a 'human story' we have punctuated this account with short biographical sketches of, and personal statements from, many of the leading participants: their lives, their struggles and this dispute are so completely entwined that they form a natural 'unity' and an appropriate part of the text.

# Chapter 1

## *The past is always with us*

Much has been written about the history of dock work and dockers organisation and it is not our intention to repeat much that can be found elsewhere.[5] Nevertheless the history of dock work and the dock unions is important for two significant reasons. First, because it is the history of a particularly exploited sector of the labour force, where poor conditions of employment and casualism were the norm until 1967 and where the struggle against such conditions, in combination with the large number of people employed on the docks, created one of the most important sections of the British working class movement. Throughout the years dockers have fought for their right to representation, to improve their conditions of employment and provide solidarity with other workers in struggle. In general terms, theirs is a history to be proud of.

But the history of dock work is important in a second more immediate sense because it informs the values of many of those from traditional dock communities. In what may be termed an 'historical, collective consciousness', personal histories are passed down from generation to generation describing and outlining what conditions on the docks were like in the past and emphasising how hard previous generations had to fight to improve things. Thus dockers and their families do not need to be told that, historically, the industry has been plagued by irregular employment patterns, casualism, inadequate health and safety cover and poor pay; that dock work is strenuous, demanding and often dirty, and that the employers have made their money out of the extreme exploitation of their labour power and by ignoring the claims of workers for better safety standards, protective clothing and the creation of a 'normal' work environment. At times these facts of working life have brought severe poverty and hardship to the dockers' families but they have also created a deep sense of community and class solidarity. Such solidarity can be

## *Jimmy Nolan*

*I was born in the Scotland Road area of Liverpool . My father was a seaman and a socialist. I first came to work on the docks in 1964 when I was 19. I had previously worked on a building site but was sacked for my activities as a shop steward. The first major strike on the port that I was involved in took place in 1967 and lasted for six weeks. This was an important strike in the Liverpool port. We were fighting to establish better rates of pay, better working conditions including the removal of the ten hour day, and the right to elect shop stewards. Winning the right to elect our own shop stewards was an important step forward in our fight for industrial democracy. I was first elected in 1967 and have been re-elected by the men every two years since then. In 1967 the Merseyside Shop Steward Committee was created so that the stewards could meet together and act collectively. An executive committee was also formed and a chair and a deputy chair elected. In 1968 Liverpool was influential in the creation of the National Port Shop Stewards Committee which was an important organisation in the establishment of an effective national rank and file movement.*

*After the 1989 dispute it appeared that the MDHC wished to destroy the shop stewards movement within the port. They resorted to derecognising those stewards who questioned their actions. Jimmy Davies and I were first derecognised in 1991 when we advocated that the men who worked at Torside should be placed on the same rates of pay as other dock workers. The fact that we had been democratically elected meant nothing to the MDHC. We were derecognised again in 1994. At the recent Commons Committee Bernard Cliffe said that we were derecognised on this occasion because they didn't believe we were doing a good job on behalf of the MDHC. We didn't realise that we were supposed to be representing them. Indeed we were delighted at the news that the company didn't believe we were working for them!*

*In 1994 the men voted against accepting contracts which removed the six hour shift system and replaced it with a twelve hour one. However they were sent letters informing them that they had to accept the contract within 90 days or they would be sacked. This was a draconian agreement from the dark ages. It is one of the bitter ironies of this dispute that 30 years ago we were fighting to remove a 10 hour day and now in 1996 we are forced to work a twelve hour day . Central to this current dispute is the abuse of industrial power backed by the Anti-Trade Union Laws.*

*I was recently at a conference where I addressed one hundred representatives of port workers from around the world. Each of them pledged that, upon their return to their own country, they would advocate support for our struggle. Our problems are being discussed throughout the world but those problems are not unique to Liverpool. The support that we have received both in Britain and throughout the world will sustain us until we gain our objective of reinstatement for all the sacked dockers.*

expressed in many large and small ways: strikes, go slows, boycotts and support for workers within and outside of the docks; but also the support for sick work mates, old dockers, families with large numbers of children or children with special needs.

In this chapter, we briefly look at the form of labour relations that has existed on the docks and the memories and oral histories of those involved in the present dispute, who are determined that there should be no return to casual working. First, then, we look at the dominant labour relations on the docks.

'Dock work' as a generic term can be a bit misleading. It gives the impression of being a uniform and unified occupation but, in reality, it applies to a range of tasks and skills performed by workers on the dock quay, in gantries above ships and within ships' holds. Until 1967, employment on the docks had been 'casual'. The system, 'casualism', required men to report at the dock-gate, a labour stand, pen or other recognised hiring point, where they would wait to be hired for an hour or half-day depending on the fluctuating labour requirements of ships, dock companies and stevedoring agencies. The men who were hired would often remain employed until the end of the particular loading or discharging operation they were involved with was completed. Those who failed to get hired either wandered the dock area looking for employment or went home until the next hiring, later that day or the following morning.

Casualism was thought to be the only appropriate method of meeting the labour requirements on the docks. Trade fluctuations were affected by economic booms and slumps, seasonal imports and exports, the tide and the weather. The dockers were also offering themselves for hire to a vast number of small and medium sized employers each under pressure to turn the ships around as quickly as possible - because a ship tied up in the docks is not earning money but is, instead, a drain on its owner's resources. Hence, quick turnarounds are, and always have been, crucial to ship owners. All this meant that on occasions there was 'bunching' of demand, when ports would be stretched in order to load and unload the vessels using the docks as quickly as possible, and periods of relative quiet when fewer workers were taken on. The result was a problem of underemployment; a large number of dockers were required to meet potential shortfalls but the rarity of these peak demands meant that the norm was more workers looking for employment than there were jobs available. It was underemployment that was the cause of poverty for dockers' families.[6] The poverty and degradation forced on dock families has been well recorded by social

## *Kevin Robinson*

*I was born and brought up in the southend dock area. My father was a docker, as was his father before him. Everyone I knew was associated with the waterfront in some way. The docks were a central part of my life as I grew up. When I left school both my father and grandfather were determined that I should work elsewhere and I was lucky enough to get an engineering apprenticeship. I was playing football with Blackburn Rovers at the time and completed my apprenticeship at Preston. When I finished though, I still wanted to go on the docks and my uncle managed to get me on in 1968, just after the end of casualism. I love working on the docks, I think I suffer from industrial claustrophobia: I hate being penned down, I like to be able to walk around and do different jobs. Even if a job is really hard, I don't mind, because I know that when the ship is ready we'll be onto something completely different. I've been a shop steward for most of my time on the docks: I hate to see people getting pushed around, especially by bosses who think they have the right to treat you like dirt. I believe we have the right to be treated decently, to work for decent pay, to get proper overalls and safety equipment and to be represented by our union and by 'our own,' those who do the work and know what it's like on the docks. If need be we have to fight to keep these things. In the last few years I've been 'derecognised' by the company on four occasions, they said I had a pathological hatred of managers - but as far as I'm concerned its the men I work with who elect me and as long as they are happy with me and 'recognise' me as their steward I'll continue to do a job for them if I can. If any of my three sons want to go onto the docks, I want them and others, to enjoy the hard fought conditions that we have won.*

commentators throughout the last two centuries. Henry Mayhew (1851),[7] Beatrice Webb (1887)[8] and Eleanor Rathbone (1904)[9] each reported with horror the poverty caused by casual working. Wilson quotes figures from the Poor Law Guardians for the post-World War One period: in 1923 West Ham guardians reported that 44% of men on relief were dockers.[10] A similar picture emerges from the 1930's. The depression had severe consequences in the docks with tonnage handled reduced substantially when compared to pre-World War One figures. Wilson spells out the consequences:

> [In the 1930's] dockland earnings were some 15% to 25% lower than in the building trade,and the reason was not poor rates of pay but underemployment. In Liverpool, for instance, the rate for a 44 hour week was 67s 4½ d, in 1931 against 42s 1d in engineering and 51s 1d in building. But in [these] trades average earnings were higher.[11]

Causalism meant it was exceptionally difficult to obtain employment for a full week; underemployment, and hence poverty, was the norm and in these circumstances there was intense competition between the men for these jobs. As Allen notes:

> Ernie Bevin, wartime Minister of Labour and General Secretary of the Transport and General Workers' Union, described Liverpool's dock road as '...the nearest thing to slave pens in Western civilisation'. Dockers would scramble - and scrap - to catch the eye of the foreman who would pick men for work with a tap on the shoulder or the feel of a muscle.[12]

Bill Hunter quotes an older docker who describes what the system meant in practice:

> Older men on the docks remember the thirties very well. The humiliation of the stands. The 'muscle feeling.' The scramble for a job. They remember the 'blue eyes' system - the whisper of 'you're staying behind' into the ear of a favoured one. The militant was isolated. The man who refused to overload a sling on the last ship was left standing.[13]

Despite the pressure dividing the men against each other, one of the most exceptional features about dock work has been that, despite the competition, there has also been a general commitment to trade unionism. The work culture promotes solidarity between dockers. The vast number of employers meant that dockers could move up and down the docks and meet and work alongside a range of other workers; the commitment to quick turnarounds meant that, after they had been hired, the gangs were in a relatively strong bargaining position, and could 'spot bargain' for a higher rate for the job. Employers were limited in their ability to control the actual work tasks being performed, with the result that there was potential for quite significant independence and autonomy, and for the dockers, collectively, to organise their employment routine and practices. Such features were structured by various unspoken rules of custom and practice which dockers would adhere to and have been shaped by their shared understanding of the history of dock work. A member of the present workforce makes a point that this history and culture is important in determining how dockers 'look after their own.'[14] Kevin Robinson started in 1968 and was gradually introduced to the work by his older colleagues:

> Because of the camaraderie they would put you to one side and show you 'this is how you do it'...they would always give you the easy part and they always nurtured you and helped you.

But custom determined that 'helping' went further than simply introducing young workers to the task of employment. It involved a range of activities that would protect fellow workers who were sick, injured or vulnerable on one count or another and generally supporting workmates who were in difficult social circumstances. Here is Kevin again:

> If [someone] had a broken hand then, because the sick pay was abysmal, you'd carry him and you carried him because...they've got families to support and you'd work twice as hard just to try and keep them on the pay roll...and they'd do that for you...[in gangs] one of you'd always get extra [for organising and being gang leader] but you always gave that to the one with the most kids...Sometimes, if there were two gangs down below, you might nominate two people from the other gang.

Thus, dock work in the period of casualism, engendered experiences which both united and divided dockers from each other, but also promoted a deep hostility to employers who were seen to benefit directly from the dockers' labour.

The outbreak of World War Two brought the need for the 'efficient' operation of the docks and rapid turnaround of ships. In these circumstances the state intervened to try and curtail the chaos of the worst features of casualism: the vast numbers of employing agents competing with each other was curtailed to some extent by forced cooperation. The vital west coast ports around Liverpool and Glasgow, which dealt with

## *Frank Lanigan*

*I'm a fourth generation docker. I was brought up next to the docks and my early memories are shaped by what it was like to work on the docks and raise a family on the uncertainties of dock wages. I know what casualism meant - no ships equals no money. My father was a union activist and Cunard banned him from working their cargoes for 6 years, he was injured in 1976 and left the industry at that point.*

*I went onto the docks in 1973, I worked in the west coast area. In 1981 I was elected shop steward. Looking back at my time on the docks I can see two distinct phases: 1973-1989 and 1989-1995. In the 1973-1989 period there were more men working, the atmosphere was livelier and better, we enjoyed the work and there was a lot of camaraderie. The shop stewards movement was strong, met regularly and represented the men to management at the various joint consultative meetings. I was on the Port Stewards Executive Committee and 'Modernisation Committee' which was the major committee overseeing the introduction and regulation of any changes to wages or working practices on the docks. In this period we were confident, well organised and respected. After 1989 there was an assault on the rank and file organisation based on the imposition of six different contracts for workers in six defined areas of the port. Management attempted to curtail the role of the stewards on the shop floor and if we undertook activities they didn't like they would derecognise us. This eventually occurred in 1991/92 and the result was that a number of inexperienced men became stewards - and management and the union steamrollered them. There was a major attack on our conditions and a deterioration in our working lives. Faced with this situation we decided to accept the 'accreditation process' so we could get in and represent our members and gradually repel the assault - but the sackings of September 1995 stopped that process.*

*We are in dispute to get the re-instatement of the 500 sacked workers - that must be our main goal. Then it's about those who want to stay in the industry working in decent conditions and those who want to leave doing so via a dignified severance scheme.*

the vast bulk of transatlantic aid and supplies, were placed under the control of the Ministry of War Transport. As Allen notes:

> [The MOWT] registered both employers and dockers. Dockers worked for a single employer, the MOWT, for the first time, with guaranteed maintenance payments for dockers 'in attendance' but unable to secure work.[15]

For other docks, the National Dock Labour Corporation was set up, a tripartite body comprising representatives of employers, the state and the trade union officials. These developments gave the unions a partial say in administering the registers (of dockers) and hence a foothold in the labour hiring process. Allen argues there were additional benefits brought in for the workers, such as the 'continuity rule' which made sure that men would remain employed in a job until it was completed. In this context Allen argues: "employers were vehemently opposed to continuity"[16]

However, Wilson suggests that continuity was brought in to try and control dockers. Acute labour shortages during the war strengthened the dockers bargaining position, and:

> There were some 30 strikes in each of the war years, in spite of Order 1305 which made strikes and lockouts illegal...Absenteeism grew as the war progressed, reaching 30% on occasions in Liverpool. (It was to counter absenteeism and the mens' tendency to walk off jobs that they did not like that the famous Continuity Rule was introduced...at the employers request).[17]

These contrasting explanations emphasise the complexity of employer-employee relationships on the docks. In a highly charged and conflictual atmosphere there is always suspicion of the employers' motives and a range of restrictive practices, customs and traditions, can only be understood against the wider rubric of class relations and antagonisms within the docks in particular and society at large.

After the war these formal labour relations and arrangements were extended to 1947 when, in June of that year, the National Dock Labour Scheme came into being. Allen outlines the main features of the 1947 scheme:

> Under the scheme, around 78,000 dockers in 86 ports became employees of the National Dock Labour Board. The scheme removed employers' freedom to hire and fire, their principal means of imposing discipline, by ending the direct relationship between dockers and individual employers or stevedoring firms, and imposed

joint control of discipline and registers through local dock labour boards. Private 'operational employers' were required to give advance notice of estimated labour requirements to the dock labour boards which served as 'holding employers', and provided 'fallback' pay for underemployed men. But casualism was not fully eliminated...few dockers were employed on a weekly basis.[18]

The scheme built on existing port institutions and incorporated regional and local differences of tradition, custom and practice. The scheme still required men to make themselves available at the hiring posts to obtain work, and those who did not obtain work were required to report to the local dock labour board's pen, to see if there was any other 'suitable work' within daily travelling distance, or to get their book stamped to qualify for fallback pay. The introduction of the scheme did not stop conflict on the docks, but, instead, initiated one of "the most turbulent periods in the history of both the port transport industry and the dockers' trade unions".[19]

Between 1949 and 1973 around 50% of dockers were involved in strikes (compared with 28% of coal miners) with an average of one strike per two employees. In terms of working days lost, the dock strikes peaked in 1954 and 1955 despite similar strike figures for 1967, 1970 and 1972. The major dock strikes were largely caused by various residues of casualism.[20]

Conflicts arose over the day to day functioning of the scheme, over health and safety, pay, overtime, working conditions and the perceived failure of the main union, the TGWU, to represent the workforce and improve the dockers' position. According to Hunter:

The Dock Labour Scheme was in fact the embodiment of conflicting forces, with the strength of the workers pushing back the power of the employers, but being controlled and checked by trade union and labour leaders. It was a framework in which the employers could maintain a base from which to regain their complete domination. Because post-war trade expanded immediately after the war, leading to almost negligible unemployment in the country as a whole, the dockers were in a much stronger position to press home their demands for an improvement in pay and conditions.[21]

The involvement and incorporation of the TGWU on local dock boards produced conflict between the union and the rank and file. One consequence was the breakaway of a large number of dockers to the 'blue union' (National Amalgamated Stevedores and Dockers - NASD), because of its apparent willingness to fight for better wages, conditions and worker representation.[22]

The post-war boom strengthened the dockers' bargaining position and led to a steady increase in their wages. The casual hiring and work system remained in place and this, in a period of a tight labour market and increased pressure from a large number of employers for a quick turnaround on ships, enabled the gangs to spot-bargain to improve the pay for particular jobs. However, working conditions remained exceptionally poor, there were no occupational pensions so men often worked beyond the age of 65, the pen hirings remained in place and the existing gang system was often difficult to penetrate for young workers: younger dockers had the disadvantages of casualism without many of the benefits that established gangs had carved out of the system. This younger generation are the older workers involved in the present dispute and their memories of casualism are almost uniformly negative (although at the time, among some sections of the workforce, casualism was defended against further state or employer interference). Their negative memories and recollections strengthen their resolve in the present lockout. At the start of the dispute many of the older dockers were uncertain how their pensions would be affected by their stand but despite this they remain the most intransigent opponents of any deal except a return to work.

These are some of the comments dockers made about the working situation prior to 1967. Billy started on the docks in 1968 but his father and older brothers worked prior to decasualisation and his memories are shaped by witnessing their experiences:

> You'd go in the pen and men would be fighting and climbing over each other's backs to get the boss to take your book [and hire you]...In fact it was that bad [in the docks] that if you were out of work the dole used to threaten you 'get a job or we'll send you down the docks'...the conditions were terrible the cargoes were open and filthy and you couldn't get a boiler suit, or mask...[there was]....one particular job...on fishmeal,...you can imagine the smell of crushed fish...and our John and Peter [his brothers] and my dad would tell us that there was times they'd get on the bus to come home and people would actually stand up and move away from them.

Irregular employment in working life, built up problems as dockers got older. Men of all ages would be on the docks and retirement at 65 did not come in on Liverpool docks until 1969. Jimmy Davies remembers that, "you actually had men of 75 and 80 still working below". Again, Jimmy

16

## *Jimmy Davies*

*I started work in 1960 when I was 18. My father was on the docks at the time and he was instrumental in getting me on. At that time they were still operating a casual system and I went into pen number 8, which dealt with all the coastal traffic to Ireland. There were about 2,000 men in that control area and the boss would wander round and put his hand on your shoulder to indicate that he'd hire you. The problem was that there was an old established gang system and it was very difficult to break into that if you were a young lad - I never really broke into the system before casualisation ended in 1967 - and so you would end up with a couple of days work and a couple of days on the dole each week. I was involved in my first dispute on my first day at work! You had 6 months probation on the docks and my dad warned me to keep my nose clean. He wasn't at all pleased when I went home that first night and told him I had walked off a ship - although I didn't have much say about anything I just followed the older blokes. I've always been in the union and I first became a steward in 1969. After the 1994 agreement Jim Nolan and myself became full-time worker representatives. I think MDHC thought they were buying us off but of course we were representing the union and the men they quickly re-recognised us and tried to make us sign new contracts and go back in the docks. This is a very important dispute. Its about casualisation and making sure there is no return to the past - that is why we must win.*

Davies, who went onto the docks in 1960, describes what working life was like:

> The conditions the men worked under were horrendous...The [hiring] system was at the whim of the boss...[sometimes] religion had a lot to do with whether you got hired...[sometimes]...it just depended on the boss's mood and there was a lot of greasing the boss's palm....The hours were incredible, they'd start at 7 in the morning and sometimes go till 7 or 10 at night and be out at 7 in the morning again...If there was no work, they stamped your book and sent you home and you'd come back the next day.

Jimmy Nolan expands on what working conditions were like:

> When I first came on the docks in 1964 it was...winter...and what I still remember clearly was the cold. You were expected to work in the rain, the snow and gale force winds and everything. There was no protective clothing, you were just expected to work in your ordinary clothes that you came and went home in. The working conditions were obnoxious, there was no protective gear of any type regardless of the job.

The iniquity of the hiring system, long hours of work, the poor working conditions and the irregularity of employment are the four elements which older dockers identify as the curse of casualism. After outlining what it was like when he started work and identifying the central problems, Jimmy Davis adds: "that's what I'm terrified of now - going back to that system". Terry has similar concerns. He also started in 1960.

> I remember the pens...and the labour officers...were like the Gestapo, controlling and ruining people's lives...When you were casual, you were a nothing, you couldn't get anything, you couldn't get a mortgage...and all that was eradicated...[in 1967, but].. it's as if it's all coming back

While Tom, who also started in 1960 made the same telling point:

> [today] they want agencies to hire you by the day, they don't want to give you pensions, no sick pay...What is happening is we are going back 30 years to 1966.

The dockers' individual and collective memories of the situation on the docks prior to 1967 contrasts sharply with their experiences and recollections of the period 1967-1989. From the mid-1960's pressure had being gradually building against the dominant form of employment in the docks industry. The shipping industry, state and dock boards were

## Herbie Hollerhead

*I'm a fourth generation docker. When I left school I went to sea until I was 21 (in 1961) and I could come onto the dock. I started in box five on the Canada dock. They still had pens then and we were herded in like cattle and picked out. I was a holdsman, you started on the quay but if you worked down below you got 9 pence more. I have never done anything else. I have only been out of work for an hour since I left school.*

*When I started, I worked with my grandfather. He remained on the dock until 1970 when he was 81, he would have continued but he was made to quit by the Port Authority. There were men up to the age of 90 still working on the docks until they finished off the older dockers around 1970.*

*The working conditions on the dock were at their best in the early seventies and these provided the best times I've had on the docks. After the abolition of the dock labour scheme in 1989 we were placed in a terrible situation, I never had a Saturday or Sunday off in 7 years. I was first placed in the general handling area and then on the Pandoro Ferries. While I was there I was elected steward, although I had always been active in the union I had never been a steward before. I was their Steward for three years and then I was a steward at the Norse Irish for four years. In the run up to the dispute we had increased the productivity on the Norse Irish by 60%, and yet we were sacked within 10 minutes of it starting. They flew in scabs from Ireland and around the country. I believe that they had been planning to get rid of us for some time.*

*The highlight of the dispute for me is the moral character of the men and the fact that they will never give in. There are 32 men on the Norse-Irish most of whom have over 30 years service. We picket every day from 7am until 9pm, everyone is involved including our wives. Since the dispute started I have found myself becoming much closer to my sons and my wife.*

*My wife and I have been on delegations together and she has been with me when I have spoken to large meetings in Liverpool. I have been on many delegations both in Britain and abroad, once the other stewards made me get a passport that is! My wife's boss is actually a scab's wife and she was talking at work about what he was doing and how she was proud of him. My wife is very quiet and didn't say anything but she went into work with her Support the Docker stickers and literature and the other women turned on the scab's wife and they now all support the dockers.*

*When I started there were 30,000 men working on the dock now there are only 500, they are making more profit then ever but they are still not satisfied. I know we are planning for a long term victory if we achieve that it will be a victory for all working people in this country as well as ourselves.*

committed to modernising the docks and the dominant form of labour relations on the docks. The development of container technology has had phenomenal social consequences. Under present social relations it has meant that it is possible to load and unload larger quantities of cargo, in shorter periods of time, using fewer dockers. For employers, such developments also promote changes to payment agreements: when ships have to be hand loaded, large numbers of dockers paid via low flat rate payments in combination with both tonnage and particular cargo bonuses are thought to encourage quick work (and hence, quick ship turn-round); in the container era, fewer dockers are needed and larger flat rates of pay are thought more suitable. In such circumstances, casualism and the traditions and culture it had created were viewed as an impediment to change and 'rational' working. The expectations and wishes of the workforce, of course, may not match any of these employer led demands.

These developments led to increasing demands for the docks to become 'modernised'. The Devlin Committee (1965) report into dock work represented the official concerns, but the dockers themselves, and especially the younger generation who had been recruited throughout the 1960's, were also an important source of change. As the 1960's progressed the terrible work and employment conditions on the docks contrasted sharply with conditions in other working class occupations. Powerful shop stewards' organisations had been built in a range of industries and they had managed to obtain improvements to wages and conditions in a period marked by what has been termed 'do it yourself' reformism (i.e. stewards would lead unofficial wildcat strikes, work to rule and overtime bans to improve conditions and would often obtain quick concessions before the union officials became involved or the negotiating machinery invoked). However, there was no stewards' system on the docks, although there was a tradition of rank and file trade unionism, and the fact that many unemployed young people were threatened with dock work emphasises both the gap that existed between conditions on the waterfront and elsewhere and the fact that this was generally recognised.

The Devlin Report led to decasualisation of dock work via a two phased modernisation programme. Phase I of the agreement ended casual employment in all registered ports in September 1967. Phase II was to be a port by port agreement which was intended to end various restrictive practices, tighten work discipline and set various productivity agreements in place. However, the 1967 Scheme neither nationalised the docks nor did it bring the various unregistered ports under the scheme; this was a major failing as the unregistered ports were to play an increasingly important role in undermining the NDLS. The introduction of the 1967 Scheme was also met with a rash of strikes as dockers in ports up and down the country stuck against various terms of the decasualistion programme. In Liverpool there was a successful six week dispute against the new imposed working conditions and for improvements to bonus payments.

1967 saw the era of casualism come to an end. It also radically improved the situation on the docks and, importantly, saw the creation of what was to become a very important and powerful shop stewards' movement. However, the modernisation programme also led to a substantial decline in the number of dockers employed both nationally and in Liverpool, as is made clear in Table 1.

| Table 1[23] | | |
| --- | --- | --- |
| **Figures of Registered Dockers** | | |
| **Year Ended** | **National Register** | **Liverpool** |
| 1947 | 79,769 | |
| 1957 | 75,700 | 16,085 |
| 1967 | 56,808 | 11,530 |
| 1969 | 49,225 | 11, 100 |
| 1971 | 43,645 | 10,427 |
| 1973 | 34,590 | 7,550 |
| 1975 | 31,884 | 7,326 |
| 1977 | 29,168 | 6,402 |
| 1979 | 25,770 | 5,202 |
| 1981 | 18,219 | 3,402 |
| 1983 | 13,813 | 2,151 |
| 1985 | 11,922 | 1,862 |
| 1989 | 9,400 | 1,100 |
| De-registration | | |

Of the 1967 strike, Billy comments:

I remember going to the meetings at the Pier head with my brothers and my dad. It was a tremendous strike, a tremendous victory.

Tom says:

[As a result of the strike] we were able to get shop stewards and be represented by them,...and, afterwards, they were euphoric years...at last we felt we were getting somewhere...getting decent conditions...having a say in things.

Ray and John spoke to us about the change they noticed after the '67 strike:

(Ray): There was a really good atmosphere, the men were good and they were confident

(John): Yes, the men you worked with made the job good...and the union were able to get us better wages, conditions, the stewards were always there if you needed them

(Ray): Yes, the steward was always there to do the business for you.

For Billy the most important element of change after 1967 was that hiring became more open and that there was an end to the scramble for work and the petty corruption that the old system produced.

The hire went from being the boss who put you on to a book system. You'd go into the control every morning [and] present yourself for work...If you were given work you'd get a green stamp and if you got no work you got a red stamp. So obviously once you'd worked and came back into the pen you had the green stamps and so you'd go to the back of the queue so the lads who had the red stamps got work...there was no 'blue eye system'...it made no odds who you were there was control systems, it was fairer and you were hired by the stamp...and the stewards were there to see it worked properly.

For Jimmy Nolan the key victory brought about by the 1967 strike was the establishment of an effective shop stewards' movement. As he notes:

After 1967 was over, and with the support and involvement of Jack Jones [then General Secretary of the TGWU] we established the Merseyside Shop Stewards' Movement. This was not the intention of the employers. They thought...that shop stewards would only act within the confines of their own area, but we wanted no part of that, so we organised a port shop stewards' committee where all the stewards would attend meetings. [we organised the length and breadth of the docks from south to north and Birkenhead] In addition, the port shop stewards elected a chair and a secretary as well as an executive committee. The first chair in 1967 was Dennis

22

Kelly and I was elected deputy chair. The first thing we did was to examine all the problems that existed in the port. We came out with a clear policy to advance pay and conditions and also to make it clear to employers that protective clothing was a necessity and we also made it clear we were not prepared to work in extremely inclement weather.

Jimmy Davies suggests the ramifications of the victory in 1967 went beyond the docks. He argues that the victory on the docks and the improvement in pay and conditions fed the confidence of other workers in Merseyside to fight for better conditions. Thus he suggests that the 1967 strike was an important landmark in the history of the entire British working class movement in the late 1960's and early 1970's. He says:

> The '67 strike was the big one when we made a real breakthrough. Obviously it was a national strike but when the other ports went back Liverpool stayed out to fight for better conditions in Liverpool and we managed to achieve that...they had a strike committee then, just like we have now..because they didn't have stewards before '67...And...there was a follow on throughout the city...you'd hear people say 'if the dockers can do it so can we', I remember a bus driver saying 'if it's good enough for the dockers it's good enough for us'...and a lot of people managed to get good pay increases on the back of what we'd achieved.

Decasualisation brought security of employment and put registered dockers in a much stronger bargaining position.

After 1967, therefore, there were a number of significant changes on the docks. Shop stewards were recognised by the employers and thus there was a significant change in their status. They were to establish an officially recognised role in expressing rank and file demands and defending and protecting dockers from management. Wages improved, safety became prioritised, protective and waterproof clothing were gradually provided as a right and the jobs were relatively secure. Some of these changes were a consequence of the fact that after 1967 dockers were permanent employees under the NDLS, but many were enshrined in negotiated agreements and were the result of better union organisation and confidence.

Furthermore, these developments were built onto the work practices and work culture of the pre-1967 era to produce an effective combination: a strong union presence protecting and defending workers' relative freedom to control the pace of work and the general functioning of the labour process. As Turnbull and Wass note:

> The problem for management was that...the system of work administration...placed considerable control over the organisation and execution of work tasks in the hands of dockers...Even containerisation, which destroyed dockers' jobs, deskilled the work of those who remained in employment, and facilitated the introduction of more systematic managerial control over the work process...was subject to powerful counter-control on the shopfloor.[24]

Of course, from the perspective of 1996, it can be seen that the new container technology has had a devastating impact on jobs in the ports. The point is, however, that rank and file strength and the dominant work culture created the conditions for resistance to its imposition. This combination was a powerful mechanism to defend dockers and enable them to retain a degree of control over their work. It certainly established dockers as one of the key sections of the working class movement in Britain. As the 1970's drew to a close it became clear that management on the docks were becoming increasingly assertive about their 'right to manage' and that this was an attitude that was to be given full backing by the new Conservative government established in office in 1979 and committed to a policy whose aim was to undermine the power of the unions.

The Tory government elected in 1979 was determined that there would be no re-run of the 1970-74 period where the Heath government's economic and social policy, and in particular its anti-union legislation, was effectively beaten by the trade union movement. The Thatcher government was determined there would be no 'U-Turn' in economic and industrial relations policy. In the field of industrial relations, the government followed what was known as the 'Ridley Plan'. This was a two-pronged strategy. First, the unions were to be dealt with one at a time rather than in a generalised assault; in particular confrontation with the 'big battalions of the labour movement', the miners and dockers for example, were to be avoided until the government was fully prepared. Second, a rolling legislative programme was to gradually restrict the 'legal' activities of unions: limiting the number of pickets, outlawing secondary action, enforcing ballots and threatening union funds, via sequestration, if any union was found guilty of breaking the law. The government from 1979 onwards more or less adhered to the tactics of the Ridley Plan, but it nevertheless remained a potentially problematic strategy: as the steel workers, hospital and local government workers, print workers and, eventually, miners and dockers, were confronted there was always the possibility that the particular dispute would command more general support and that the government would be defeated. The massed pickets during the steel strike, the confrontations at Warrington over Eddy Shah's attempts to break the National Graphical Association, the threat during the miners' strike that first the dockers and then the pit deputies would join the dispute, the struggle at Wapping, the national walk out in the docks over the abolition of the NDLS - each of these events had within it the possibility of defeating the government. That each went down to defeat was less to do with Thatcher's invincibility or the terminal decline of the union movement but more to do with the trade union leaders' adherence to the (anti-union) laws and their unwillingness to call for, and support, solidarity action.

Looking back at these events many of the dockers are clear about what was happening and what should have been done. Tom suggests that the problem set in during the mid-1970's. "We were on top then" he claims, but "we got blasé". Terry suggests the 'problems' set in during the last Labour government when workers "were told 'Don't rock the boat' or the Tories will get back, and we waited and we let their side get on top". He continues:

> [after the Tories were elected in 1979] the first time they brought in their anti-union laws we should have been out, the TUC should have called us out and that would have been that.

On the possibility of joint action with other groups Derek suggests:

> we would have come out with the miners if we'd had have a chance...but it was obvious that if anybody had taken secondary action during the miners' strike they would have sequestrated their funds and the T&G was terrified of losing its assets...but we knew after the miners they were coming for us.

Brian argues:

> we could see what was happening attacking different groups one at a time and we knew they were coming for us... in 1985 we had an opportunity. They were bringing coal in via non-scheme ports and we came out...but they weren't ready and they backed down they just caved in and were apologising and everything...they didn't want to fight us all at once...but that was a real chance.

While in more strategic terms Terry argues:

> workers are just a big family and we've got to stick together - bosses

do, they always stick together. If a boss finds another boss who is being attacked, he's there helping him out...[But]..one of the sad things...is where is the TUC, where are the union leaders? Why aren't they out backing us when we're fighting? The CBI speaks for the bosses, the TUC should speak for us.

As we have noted, then, dockers are very aware of their own past and this has shaped many of their attitudes to the present struggle. Their 'collective memory' has three main elements: first, a recognition of the reality of casual work practices with long hours, poor wages and bleak working conditions; second, their tradition of community and class solidarity and, third, their memories of effective and strong rank and file trade unionism and, at the very least, suspicion or mistrust of the trade union hierarchy. By 1989 the anticipated confrontation arrived when the government announced the abolition of the NDLS. The consequences of abolition are addressed in Chapter 2.

# Chapter 2

## *Abolition of the National Dock Labour Scheme (NDLS)*
## *and the return of casual working*

The direct roots of the present dispute are to be found in the settlement reached at the end of the six week strike in 1989 over the abolition of the National Dock Labour Scheme (NDLS).[25] Port employers, at registered ports, had been demanding the scheme's abolition for a number of years. In 1985, for example, port employers approached the government with this demand. However, at the time, the government was still recovering from its confrontation with the miners and put off abolition until after the 1987 election.[26] Nevertheless, the government and employers did, however, start to make plans to beat a port blockade during any future confrontation.[27]

For the port employers, the NDLS was an anachronism: it undermined their 'right to manage' their ports in any way they saw fit; it promoted 'rigid' as opposed to 'flexible' working; it was expensive, rule-laden and allowed trade union militants to disrupt working arrangements. They argued that, in an increasingly competitive environment, ports should be free from the restrictions of the NDLS and allowed to employ whoever they want, in whatever conditions they thought appropriate and for 'realistic' wage rates. They demanded the abolition of the NDLS so they could return to more casual employment relations, break down rigid job demarcations and allow the scheme ports to compete with non-scheme ports in Britain and also European ports. The purpose of abolition was essentially to restore managerial control within the industry; the means of achieving this were to redefine 'dock work', to break traditional patterns of work and behaviour and to remove ex-registered dockers and trade union militants from the waterfront.

Eventually, with government and port authorities armed with an eight week strategy to sit out any dock strike,[28] the government published a Bill to abolish the NDLS on 7 April 1989. When the Bill was published dockers at both Liverpool and Tilbury immediately walked out on strike. In response, Ron Todd, then General Secretary of the TGWU, pleaded with the dockers to return to work: the unofficial action was illegal and the port employers immediately intimated their intention to use the law against the TGWU in the case of any unofficial dispute, or against any strike against the NDLS which affected them! They claimed the dockers grievance was with the government and, therefore, a strike at the ports would be illegal 'secondary action'. Faced with this situation Ron Todd, and the Broad Left dominated TGWU National Executive, prevaricated. They argued that the scheme could not be saved and that, instead, they would have to reach a new agreement with the government and the employers. To progress this idea, Todd sent three written requests to the employers asking for a meeting, but each was rejected. Now the TGWU decided to call a ballot for strike action, but they were worried about the form the question should take: they decided to take legal advice on the wording of the question on the ballot and to see if action at the ports could, in fact, be deemed illegal secondary action. The strike ballot was held in early May 1989 and 74.3% of dockers voted for strike action.[29] Todd and the TGWU National Executive then waited for the High Court to pass judgment on whether the strike would be illegal, only to find that the Court considered it to be a political dispute and, hence. that it would be illegal to take action against the port employers. The TGWU immediately appealed against the decision and 10 days later the Law Lords informed the TGWU they could strike. Now, however, the employers appealed and obtained an injunction against strike action: the TGWU again called off the strike until this issue could be cleared.

Faced with the TGWU leadership's inaction, the National Port Shop Stewards' Committee, comprising stewards at all registered ports, called an immediate walk-out and 2,000 dockers from Liverpool, Tilbury, Bristol, Lowestoft and Newport came out on strike. Todd immediately appealed to them to go back to work and, after a week, only Liverpool and Tilbury remained out. However, respecting a call for 'unity', Liverpool and Tilbury voted to return to work until the entire dock workforce at registered ports was called out. Eventually the Law Lords declared a strike would be legal but now the TGWU decided to re-ballot for strike action. They did this in June and July 1989 and there was another resounding vote for strike action.[30] By now, though, the Bill abolishing the NDLS having been rushed through Parliament became law and, with this backing and in the face of union prevarication, the employers went on to the offensive. At Tilbury the stewards were sacked and dockers at other ports were sent

DIRECT LINE: (01375) 852499

14th April, 1995

PORT OF
# TILBURY
LONDON

PORT OF TILBURY LONDON L1

NEPTUNE HOUSE
TILBURY FREEPORT
TILBURY, ESSEX RM18 7EH
SWITCHBOARD: (01375) 852200
FACSIMILE: (01375) 852280

Dear

I am pleased to confirm our offer of employment as a **Cargo Assistant** with Port of Tilbury Operating Services Ltd., a wholly owned subsidiary of the Port of Tilbury London Ltd.

The terms and conditions of your employment are set out below:-

- Employment will be on a sessional basis and will terminate at the end of each session. The duration of the session will be determined by the work requirement. Regular work is not guaranteed and the amount of work will fluctuate.

- Since each engagement will terminate automatically at the end of each individual session of work and there is no obligation upon either side to offer or accept further engagements, no notice is required to bring this arrangement to an end.

  When work is not provided you will not be regarded as continuing in employment for any purpose.

- There will be no basic salary. Remuneration will be paid on a monthly basis in arrears, and will be calculated according to the number of hours worked in the preceding month. The hourly rate of pay will be £6.00 except that between the hours of 10.00 p.m. and 06.00 a.m., at weekends and on public holidays, the hourly rate of pay will be £9.00. A minimum payment equivalent to three hours' attendance will apply. Payment will be made by bank credit transfer and it will be necessary for you to provide us with details of your bank account if we do not already hold them.

  PAYE Tax and National Insurance contributions, where appropriate, will be deducted directly from your salary.

- The appointment confers no entitlement to annual leave, nor to paid sick leave.

- You will not be eligible for membership of the Company's pension fund.

- No employment with any previous employer will count as continuous employment with the Port of Tilbury for the purposes of the Employment Protection (Consolidation) Act, 1978 or for any other purpose.

29

You accept the liability to drive the Port's vehicles and vehicles hired by them. Therefore, you are required to hold a current driving licence.

The nature of the employment is such that we will need to reach you by telephone. It is essential therefore that you make available a telephone number on which you may be readily contacted.

You will be required to undertake such mechanical equipment training as is deemed necessary to achieve the maintain the prescribed levels of competency.

You will be required to comply at all times during any period of employment with all rules, regulations and instructions which apply to employees at the Port of Tilbury and which may be issued to you from time to time.

Should you have any grievances relating to your employment you should raise them with Mr. Alec Faraway, the Executive Director of the Company.

You will be provided with the necessary items of protective clothing.

Discount meals will be available at the staff canteen on production of a canteen card.

If you would prefer to confine your seasonal employment to the Grain division, we will happily respect your wish. If on the other hand you would like to take advantage of additional work opportunities in the Conventional division, we would be pleased to consider you. In either event, it would greatly assist us if you could complete the attached form so that we may know your preference and range of skills.

If you accept employment on these conditions, will you please sign and return the attached copy letter to me at Neptune House.

Yours sincerely,

**John Wollaston**
**Head of Personnel Services**

Encl.

*Photostat 1: A Tilbury docker's casual contract*
*(note particularly the marked terms and conditions.)*

letters stating they would be dismissed unless they returned to work. After three weeks the only dockers remaining on strike were at Bristol and Liverpool. After another three weeks, and with Liverpool now alone, the Merseyside workforce decided to return to work. As Brian says, in these circumstances:

Liverpool was abandoned to lead the fight more or less alone and we couldn't do that, we were doomed.

Ex-docker Larry Cavanagh describes the return to work:

When we had to go back in 1989 we marched back. That was something we had never done before and something we picked up from the miners. [31]

The abolition of the NDLS was a significant defeat for the dockers and the TGWU. The left-wing leadership of the union, following a strategy of strict adherence to anti-union laws, had allowed employers to isolate and victimise trade union militants, tear up the NDLS agreements and return the ports to casual working.

In the aftermath of the dispute the industry was marked by three trends: first, dockers left in substantial numbers and between 1989 and 1992 around 80% of dockers left the industry;[32] second, the TGWU was completely marginalised in most ports, with many of its best militants forced out;[33] and third, 'casualisation', a mixture of part-time employment, 'flexible' work patterns and the euphemistically termed 'multi-skilling' (though in reality often a deskilling of work tasks) became extensive throughout the industry. A port worker at Tilbury sent the Liverpool dockers a copy of his (post abolition) contract with the warning that it was a fate that awaited a future generation of Liverpool workers if they were unsuccessful in their dispute (see Photostat 1).

As in other ports, immediately after abolition the number of dockers on the Liverpool waterfront declined substantially. As the Merseyside Port Shop Stewards' Committee note:

Between 1989 and 1995 the port operative labour force employed by MDHC ...[was]...reduced from over 1,100 to less than 500.[34]

Among these redundancies were many shop stewards and union activists who left the industry with severance payments rather than work in the new environment. Nevertheless, Liverpool remained the exception to the national picture in so far as the union remained in place and was fully recognised by MDHC. Some stewards stayed and took on the task of rebuilding their organisation and the morale and confidence of the

# *Mike Carden*

*My father and all my uncles worked on the docks. I left school in 1970 when I was 16 and my father got me a start in the main offices of the port authority in town. It was only when I was 18 that I could transfer to the docks themselves. I got a job in the clerical section. For many dock workers this was seen as a promotion for their sons.It wasn't labouring and therefore seen as 'getting on'. The docks was a magnificent place to work in the 1970's. There was a great sense of community and family. No matter how cliché ridden that sounds, in those days there was a real sense of security.*

*I remember the day that the NDLS was abolished clearly. It was a beautiful spring day April 6th 1989 and it left a lasting impression on me. In many ways it symbolised how things were to change. I was working in the container bay. A combination vessel was being worked, it had a ro-ro (roll-on, roll-off) facility and could also be loaded over the side. We have intercoms and radios in the office on the container bay so that we can listen in on the work being carried out for safety reasons. We could hear the ship's foreman shouting at the superintendent to stop this truck or to stop this loading. He said 'there is too much happening here there is going to be an accident'. The superintendent replied by insisting that the work should continue. Shortly after there was an accident when a stow of timber moved in the hatch. One of our people was killed and a number of others injured. As was custom in these circumstances the workforce prepared to leave work at 12 noon. This was done both as a mark of respect to the man who had been killed and also so that certain things that are required by law could happen i.e. an investigation into what happened. Well the dock company stopped our pay for that day. They weren't interested in showing respect to the dead dock worker. Rather they were running around telling people not to go home and threatening them with disciplinary action if they did. That same afternoon the headline in the <u>Echo</u> informed us that the National Dock Labour Scheme had been abolished.*

*It is this arrogance and inhumanity that MDHC has brought to this present dispute. However I think that it has been their undoing. They have been shocked by the solidarity of the Liverpool dockers. They have been absolutely shocked in my opinion by our dignity and the way in which we have conducted the struggle and engendered the support of people. We have brought union presidents and activists together. We held an international conference which brought rank and file members and union officials from across the world face to face. We have achieved so much. It's been a vindication of the ability of working class people to organise themselves.*

workforce. As Jimmy Nolan said:

> On the first day back after the abolition of the NDLS I was summoned to the manager's office where I was told that I had to sign the employment contract or leave the industry with £35,000. When I said that I wanted to speak to the managers and have a sight of the new contract to see how signing would affect my right to act as a negotiator, I was told that they were not prepared to do this. I knew things would be bad then, but I wanted to stay in the industry so I signed the contract.

Kevin argues that he felt there was a duty on the remaining stewards to show the workforce that they (personally) were not broken and defeated and that the fight for decent conditions continued despite the huge setback that had been suffered. As he says:

> The dock company split us up into six areas...they sent us letters threatening...if you don't go here or do this you'll be sacked...they had spin doctors telling them "this is how you deal with them, you take everything away from them, you manage"...so where we had always done things by negotiation, by arbitration, that was all taken away...[in these circumstances] some of the men couldn't stomach it and left the industry, that was their choice...but we still had a shop stewards' movement, Liverpool had stayed out longest and we had stayed together...so there were still possibilities for us...They tried to degrade us...tried to smash us down, affect our morale...and I spent a lot of time trying to convince people to stay in the industry...telling them we would have our day...and trying to challenge the bosses in all sorts of ways to show the men the fight goes on...Gradually things...came back, we'd have a laugh...when they put us on the brush, well you can only brush up so many times, so we'd have a laugh, muck about and I'd argue for proper boiler suits..masks...more brushes...and if it didn't happen we stopped..I'd tell the lads if we haven't got the tools we don't do it..so..stand still...and when we got the boiler suit, gloves and mask I demanded somewhere to change...somewhere to put my clothes. So it was an on-going thing...and when lads saw me doing that they said "he hasn't lost the fight"...and it helped our confidence.

Nevertheless, both workers and managers knew that the balance of forces had swung dramatically in the management's favour. As Kevin indicated, on the day they went back the entire workforce were put 'on the brush', set to sweeping the docks and warehouses throughout the port. Further, their job title changed, all employees were now to be known as port operations workers, shortened by MDHC to POWs. The symbolism of both acts was not lost on those returning to work. Tony described the situation:

> The first day back [after the 1989 dispute] everyone was given a brush...there were hundreds of brushes lying there...they were making a point...they changed our job title...to POWs...these were the symbols...I knew they were out to do business...which they did do...they worked out on the workforce right up to...1994 when they imposed...the new contracts.

The relative control dockers had over their work prior to 1989 meant that, although the job was strenuous, dirty and often dangerous, they nevertheless enjoyed it. This changed after 1989. The lack of control, the increase in work hours and the general demoralisation fed a feeling of despair, stress, anxiety and general lack of job satisfaction. Billy said:

> I loved the job...but it got terrible...the last six months before the dispute were the worst six months of my life on the docks.

These changes are perhaps best emphasised in relation to the increasing use of written warnings against workers with previously clean disciplinary records. Tony, a shop steward, claimed: "...there were mass disciplinings, in one week we had 129 people disciplined". Tony himself told us:

> Before the dispute I had never been disciplined in my 22 years on the docks, in one year I went from no disciplines to a final written warning for life. I lost my yearly bonus and everything.

Another docker we talked to had been put on a final warning for life because he had not answered the telephone on his rota day off !

There is little doubt that, for the dockers, working life became more draconian, more punitive and more stressful after the 1989 dispute and that worker representation declined significantly. Yet, one of MDHC's consistent refrains during this dispute is that they are not an anti-union company. As evidence they point to the fact that Liverpool is the only port in Britain where the TGWU remained recognised after 1989. While this is true it nevertheless needs to be examined in more detail. The settlement that was reached in Liverpool after the 1989 dispute was stacked in MDHC's favour- they would now call the shots, determine the conditions of work and introduce subcontracting whenever they felt it necessary. They were determined, in other words, to assert their 'right to manage'.

## *Terry Teague*

*I started on the docks in 1967 when I was 15 and I've worked there ever since. My grandfather was a docker and he got me an application form, I was interviewed and taken on by a stevedore company. There were a lot of young people starting at the same time. For a young man it was one of the best jobs in the world. You worked hard but there wasn't the regimentation and clocking on that there was in other large industries. Although the pay wasn't very good, there was a great deal of camaraderie and friendship.*

*I became a steward in 1972 and I've been involved in a number of disputes, but they were always justified: we were fighting for decent conditions, rates of pay, hours of work, holiday entitlements, a good pension scheme and the right to belong to a trade union. The shipping and dock companies were making vast profits from the fruits of our labour and it was right that we shared in that. We also felt as if we were part of a wider movement and so we've always offered solidarity to other workers.*

*After the abolition of the Dock Labour Scheme in 1989 people were demoralised but it was not immediately clear in Liverpool how drastic the changes would be. However the activists knew what was coming. The abolition of the scheme was a political decision taken by the Tories, it enabled the employers to turn the clock back and attack all the progress on decent working conditions and pay that had been made. Although the union hadn't been de-recognised in Liverpool the tactic taken by the employers was to focus on the local officials and try and destroy the shop stewards' and rank and file movements. This became clear after the imposition of new contracts in 1994. After this time any steward who actively opposed the company was derecognised. The TGWU was afraid of losing recognition, as in other ports, and was more concerned with maintaining this than challenging the company over the deteriorating working conditions.*

*For me the high point of this dispute was the first international conference with the attendance of 18 countries and 55 delegates. It represented fruition of all the hard work put in by all those who travelled abroad building support. It was a clear demonstration of how effective the international campaign has been.*

Recognition of the TGWU did not undermine that strategy, it was part of it. The history of rank and file militancy in Liverpool was a threat to the new managerial strategy but the TGWU had the potential to hold back and control militants in the port. For MDHC, therefore, the strategy was to incorporate the TGWU, at least at the local level, into their project for re-making the Liverpool docks as a profitable, trouble-free port. Of course this was never the TGWU's objective but it is also clear that the union had its own agenda which could make it vulnerable to MDHC threats. In particular it was important that they maintained an official presence in at least one port. Recognition at Liverpool rightly had to be defended but at times this led the local officials to act as 'industrial policemen', dissipating workers' anger, refusing to take industrial action and threatening the dockers that if they did not comply with management's requests they would be sacked and the Port of Liverpool would become another Hull, Tilbury, Bristol or Southampton- a port dominated by casual employment and with no union presence. As Billy says:

> Everytime they [MDHC] wanted to do something, or change something you'd get a letter threatening you with the sack if you didn't go along with them and, honest to God, about a week later we'd get a letter from the union [locally] saying the exact same thing...apart from the different letter heading you'd swear they'd been written by the same person.

As Bob complains:

> We [the Torside workforce] asked for a ballot [for industrial action] on numerous occasions, but we were consistently turned down.

Mike argues that the union was constrained by a combination of anti-union legislation and the generally anti-union atmosphere in modern Britain, but that:

> the local official wasn't very good...he was too soft...[and]...he had too cosy a relationship with MDHC.

As the stewards have argued:

> Between 1992 and 1995, MDHC made repeated threats of dismissal if their demands were not enforced. The local TGWU Official often repeated these threats.[35]

As part of their strategy of incorporation MDHC offered to employ two recognised and established shop stewards as full-time permanent union convenors: Jimmy Nolan became convenor and Jimmy Davies became deputy convenor. It is important to emphasise that a convenor system had never existed in Liverpool docks before and this was a MDHC initiative. Both Jimmy Nolan and Jimmy Davies are quite clear in their own minds that it was MDHC's intention to get two respected officials who could keep a lid on the workforce. Both were equally determined from the start that they should use their position to represent dockers and re-build the union rank and file organisation. As Jimmy Davies says:

> after a period, it wasn't even 12 months, they de-recognised the two of us because they thought we weren't carrying out the policies of the company...they thought they were putting us in to do that...but we weren't elected as convenors to represent the company we were there to represent the labour force...so we were putting leaflets in...the six areas that the company had split the docks into to try and keep them together...whenever they were having a meeting we went along...wage negotiations we were always in...when they brought one area in we went in with them, when they brought another area in we went with them...so we got de-recognised.

Jimmy Nolan notes:

> When we were de-recognised we looked at them in dismay. I said you can't de-recognise us we have been democratically elected and you have got to abide by the nature of English society. Maggie Thatcher is telling everyone that we live in a democratic society so how can you de-recognise us? But they de-recognised us anyway, which proves there is no such thing as industrial democracy and it also proves that our opposition was a threat to MDHC.

Both told us:

> At the recent Parliamentary Committee [investigating the dispute] Bernard Cliffe argued that he didn't believe that we were doing a good job on behalf of the company - we never realised that unions were supposed to act on behalf of the company.

The final example of MDHC's attitude to worker representation concerns their dealings with shop stewards and their new attitude to workers' meetings, joint union-management committees and existing negotiated agreements. In the post-1989 atmosphere MDHC gradually operated a policy of de-recognising stewards they did not like, hindering stewards from holding meetings with their members and with each other, of ending joint committees and generally breaking down the well established apparatus of consultation and negotiation that had previously existed. From 25 July 1992 the company informed the union that the 12 elected TGWU stewards were to be derecognised. As a result, proper union representation for the dockers was absent from the port for over 12 months.[36] As Jimmy Davies says:

> stewards were de-recognised [by the company]...they hindered how we worked...safety committees disappeared...you could see them breaking the structures down.

By September 1993, with the company wishing to impose the new contracts, they decided to re-recognise stewards, but any member wishing to stand was expected to sign a note of accreditation from the company. The stewards were of the opinion that this unduly restricted their abilities to adequately represent their members. Despite their concerns, as the Stewards note:

> a ballot for the election of TGWU representatives took place. This election was unique in as much as MDHC insisted that it be a secret postal ballot, paid for by the Company. More important, an asterisk was marked on the ballot paper against the name of any candidate who refused to sign the Company's note of accreditation. Consequently, the election was opposed by TGWU 6/601 Branch [the main dockers' branch], as per the rules of the Union, but the wishes of the Branch were over-ruled by the local TGWU Docks Official.[37]

This event, perhaps more than any other, shows MDHC's real attitude to worker representation. They were in favour of recognition to the extent that it enabled them to further their managerialist aims, that it dissipated worker anger and that it was contained within tightly demarcated limits set by the company. What they would have ideally liked was a 'company union' but even compliant local TGWU officials were unable to go that far. For the local TGWU officials the aim was to maintain the union's presence in the port and that meant avoiding confrontation with MDHC or damaging their 'good relationship' with the company. In many instances this produced a coincidence of interests between the company and the union officials. In essence it was the local operation of an increasingly common official trade union strategy: of appealing to employers to let them represent their workforce in negotiations and agreements - a strategy that has led to increasing inter-union rivalry over the last few years. Such concerns are also apparent in statements from trade union officials and some Labour Party M.P.'s that the dock dispute is now hurting the company - and that this should not be the aim of trade union activity in the 1990's ! [see, for example, Mass Meeting 6 September 1996]. For the dockers in the port, however, such strategies left them open to attacks on their working conditions, pay and their general representation regime. It created a gap between the dockers and their local union officials, and it was into this gap that rank and file organisation was gradually able to move and, hence, reassert itself.

Thus, over time, the tradition of trade union rank and file organisation was salvaged by the workforce throughout the complex. Partly this returned as the workforce regained their confidence. It was also a result of the hard work and dedication put in by the shop stewards, fighting to regain their right to represent their workmates. And it was partly the result of a conscious strategy, adopted whenever circumstances allowed, to move experienced union activists into work areas where the union was weakest. For example, immediately after the 1989 dispute Kevin went into the general cargo area. After a few months MDHC asked for eight people to transfer to work on the Pandoro Ferries and although Kevin didn't want to move it was decided, after discussion with the other stewards, that this would help rebuild the union organisation in that sector. One consequence was that when, in 1990, Pandoro tried to use casual labour to do dock work, there was a solid dispute in the sector, dockers stormed the Pandoro ferry and were involved in a running battle with the police: from being one of the weaker union sections within the complex the workers in the Pandoro had become one of the most militant in the fight to defend jobs and conditions.

The working environment and situation was made worse via a number of incremental changes to work practices and labour recruitment. From 1989 the stewards found themselves fighting a process of creeping casualisation and, in 1991, MDHC subcontracted essential labour tasks to a company (Torside Ltd) who employed workers on different rates of pay and working conditions from the main MDHC workforce.

Torside Ltd was set up by a former dock worker, James Bradley, who used his severence money from 1989 to set the company up. Part of the severence agreement in operation in 1989 prohibited ex-dockers from undertaking any dock work in the future. Thus Torside was formed, with full MDHC backing and with MDHC fully aware of James Bradley's previous employment record and activity, in a manner which broke severence rules.

Torside Ltd was subcontracted to provide a range of tasks throughout the Merseyside complex: they were an *essential* part of the workforce providing labour that was necessary for the smooth functioning of the

39

docks. Some stewards were unhappy at this decision and clearly argued that this was part of an attack on the working conditions throughout the port. But under pressure from the local TGWU full-time official the stewards reluctantly agreed to let Torside recruit their workforce. The port stewards tried to maintain a role in the selection process and were partially successful in their efforts. One of the ironies of the present dispute is that the Torside workers were very often the sons of dockers working in Seaforth, making the chances of any initial scabbing unlikely. Further, the stewards obtained an undertaking from MDHC that the Torside workforce would not work in any of the areas wholly owned by MDHC. However, while the dockers managed to retain a role in recruitment of the new workforce at Torside, they were not recruited on the same pay and conditions as other dockers. Initially, management claimed this was because the Torside men were undergoing an apprenticeship, but their wages and conditions never caught up with workers in the rest of the docks. Mick revealed that:

> when we started...the stewards were told we'd get these contracts, get trained up and then when jobs came up [in the rest of the complex] we'd get moved and get the better conditions...it never happened.

While John explained:

> it was like an apprenticeship...after two or three years of training we'd get the same wages as the others...it never materialised.

Indeed the Torside workforce was increasingly used throughout the docks complex working beside other dockers, doing exactly the same tasks but for less money and with poorer 'work benefits.' John stated that:

> ...we never got sick pay,...we never got holiday pay...I was working alongside all the old dockers,...we were doing the same job as them, but we were picking up £135 a week and they were picking up £250.

As Chris says:

> we were used as a wedge, to bring in casualisation, throughout the docks...they [former Registered Dock Workers] would train us up and then we'd be used to do their jobs.

Bobby Morton describes how the policy of gradually extending Torside's activities occurred:

> After 1989 MDHC operated 6 areas, each with its discrete workforce. About 14 months before the dispute they came to the

workforce at the Seaforth Timber Terminal and told them there wasn't enough work and that there was a shortage of men in the general cargo area. Out of 67 men in the timber terminal they removed 47. Although they said it was entirely voluntary, the threat was that if you didn't go the timber terminal would shut down in 6 months. But of course, as soon as a ship came into the timber area they were 47 men short and they brought Torside onto the area. Torside never left, and the significance is that the timber terminal is fully owned by MDHC.

It is clear, then, that the Torside company were being used as a mechanism to bring increasingly casualised work practices into the Merseyside complex, to use Chris's words they were the 'wedge of casualisation'. It is also clear that the Torside workforce was an essential part of the port labour force and that MDHC's operations and commitments could not be fulfilled without the use of Torsiders. The Torside workforce were part and parcel of MDHC's labour force: they were recruited at interviews held in MDHC premises, were trained at MDHC training sessions, worked on ships brought to the port by MDHC and were part of the labour force that re-established Liverpool as a profitable port. As Bobby Morton notes:

> All the negotiations to establish Torside were done by MDHC directors. All the interviews for people who went to work for Torside were conducted by MDHC personnel in MDHC's main building. All the medicals...were done by MDHC's own doctor.

While Tony Melia said:

> I was interviewed by MDHC and as far as I'm aware all my training was paid for by MDHC.

Against this background one of the more distasteful aspects of MDHC's campaign against the dockers during the dispute has been to deny any responsibility for the Torside dockers or to include them, or their representatives, in any discussions aimed at resolving the dispute.

In general terms the situation in the docks declined even more after 1994 with the imposition of new work contracts for the majority of dockers (those directly employed by MDHC). These contracts represented the clearest statement of labour casualisation and had significantly deleterious consequences on the dockers, their families and, in its widest sense, their social life. The contracts were marked by two significant features. First, hours of work were to be calculated over a three week period (of 117 hours), and second, daily hours at work could vary depending on management's requirements and the needs of shipping schedules. Workers could work anything between four and twelve hours a day and often would be unsure of their working hours when they left their homes to go on shift. Dockers have found that the new contracts meant they could work six consecutive twelve hour days before receiving a 'rota day off' in mid-week when friends and family are at jobs and children at school. Alternatively, if work was slack and dockers had worked longer hours earlier in their three week cycle they would be sent home after four hours, thus reducing their chances of obtaining overtime payments. As Mike Carden notes, "our people suffered wage cuts of anything between £3,000 and £8,000" a year. Men came off night shift straight onto their rota day and so had to sleep through their day off. Finally, even on days off the men must be prepared to go into work and so are expected to be besides their phone. As Doreen makes clear:

> We have phone calls practically on a daily basis, altering his [her husband's] shift. 7 a.m. to 3 p.m. will be changed to 7 a.m. to 7 p.m., 3 p.m. to 11 p.m. can become 11 a.m. to 11 p.m. or nights. The day before a rota day off, they can ring and change your shift to 12 hour nights, then your day off becomes a sleep day. We get calls on his day off, asking him to work or to change the next days shift. Bank Holidays, you are expected to work 12 hours, but your day in lieu you get 7 hours pay. We have had a call when he has been in bed less than 4 hours after a 12 hour shift...if you are out when they ring, they ask where you were as though you are accountable, had no right to be out and should be available 168 hours per week.

Susan described some of the effects these actions had on family life:

> the shifts were terrible, they changed them all the time. He [her husband] was coming home after twelve hour shifts and going straight to bed, he never saw the kids...they were taking everything from him. They would even leave messages with my children telling them they were changing the shift patterns...we never had holidays...we never went out anymore.

While Marie argues:

> We have 3 children, one with learning disabilities. It has proved to be very traumatic, especially the last 18 months when the current contracts were imposed. We never saw my partner, he was constantly working overtime, his rota days changed from Saturday

and Sunday so that he was off during the week, when we were all at work and school.

In these conditions family relationships become strained. John noted that:

there were weeks when I'd work twelve hours a day 7 days a week...I'd never see my family...never see the kids...It was hard on my girlfriend, I was coming home in bad moods, you know batty and if my tea wasn't on the table when I got in...I had no right to be annoyed about it, it wasn't her fault, but it was just the way work made you.

While Doreen claimed her husband has gone through:

a personality change so noticeable that neighbours, friends and family have noticed and commented on it.

Susan remarked that many of her friends and neighbours thought she and her husband were in the process of splitting up. She said:

we used to go out and have a laugh with friends and family...but it all stopped. We just stopped going out, eventually people stopped 'phoning and they started to think we had a problem at home - you know with each other.

For Derek the new contracts meant "you were like a serf to them".

Although the dockers may have directly suffered, the stresses and strains of casual working have affected entire families. As Doreen notes the imposed lifestyle has had "health effects; insomnia, loss of appetite, low spirits and stress" are increasingly a feature of dock family life. The pressures casual working creates are aptly summarised by Irene:

you can't get a mortgage on casual labour, you don't get casual bills...you can't eat casually, so what's with this casual labour?

From 1989 the Liverpool dockers and their families have suffered as a result of a developing work casualisation process. Such forms of work impinge on all areas of family and social activities - where life becomes totally dominated by, and subordinate to, the dictates of work and the company's whims. It is this feature, in combination with the history of strong rank and file trade union organisation that explains why dock families have been willing to fight for twelve months to retain jobs and improve working conditions in the port.

# *Doreen McNally*

*I was born in Liverpool, my father was a docker and all my mum's brothers were dockers. When I was a child everyone I knew was either a docker or a seafarer and so all my childhood memories are all based around the dock community. My father was badly injured on the docks and I think this was part of the reason I went into nursing. At the time there was no union for nurses, only the Royal College of Nursing which you could only join when you qualified. My father had always been a strong trade unionist and believed everyone should be in a union, he contacted someone in NUPE and we arranged a meeting with some of my colleagues. I was one of the first nurses in Liverpool to join a real union.*

*My husband joined the docks in 1968. Before this dispute, and the new contracts, we had a decent standard of living. We weren't just living Monday to Friday and I don't apologise for that- everyone should be entitled to that. However after 1989 things just got progressively worse on the docks. The dock company continually eroded the working conditions and split the workforce up into six small units in an attempt to divide and rule. My husband no longer enjoyed going to work. Torside was brought in to provide cheap labour and my husband no longer felt his job was secure. The 1994 contracts were inhuman. They were supposed to have their shifts set a year in advance but instead they only got them one week in advance and these were then subject to change at a few hours notice. On one occasion the company phoned our house 17 times in two hours. As a result, our family life was destroyed, my husband was continually tired and depressed.*

*I have never been involved in a dispute on the docks before but this one is totally different. There had never been a women's support group before but the women were so angry we decided to form one: when the dock board intrude on your family life they involve you; not only did they mistreat the men but they mistreated the families. We want to show them that we will not have our lives held to ransom by the dock company.*

# Chapter 3

## *The Women of the Waterfront*
## *(WOW)*

As we noted in the last chapter, growing work casualisation in the post-1989 period had an impact on the dockers but also on their family and social lives. Jeanette reflects the experiences of many when she describes how her family was affected:

> I was virtually existing as a single parent. Our sons rarely saw their father as he went to work before they woke and they were in bed when he returned. He left home at 6 a.m. and did not return before 10 p.m. Weekend work became compulsory. Fifteen hour days left him with no energy, he would come home, eat his meal and go to bed. We didn't talk, we had no social life, his whole life revolved around work. Holiday weeks, which were booked in advance to try to get some time with the children when they were off school, were cancelled with no prior notice. In short, life became hell.

This was a common picture of family life in dock communities in the run up to the recent dispute and this is one reason why, for the first time in a dock dispute, the wives, partners and mothers of dockers have felt the need to form their own group and take a fully active role in the fight for jobs and better conditions. The women's group was formed in the second week of the dispute and adopted the title 'The Women of the Waterfront'. They have been involved in all aspects of the struggle: fund raising, participating on national and international delegations, picketing the dock gates, as well as undertaking less conventional activities such as singing their adopted song, 'Big River' outside the homes of scabs and senior management figures in MDHC.

## Sue Mitchell

*I was born and brought up in Crosby. My dad did not work on the docks but worked in transport. I married Colin 21 years ago and at that point I gave up work to concentrate on my home and family. Colin has been involved in disputes on the docks before but I've always felt they were his affairs - I've always supported his decisions and we have always been a strong union family but I've never been involved in any way. This time things were different. The new work regime and the bosses' attitudes since the new contracts were imposed have affected the entire family: MDHC determined when we could go out, when Colin could see the children, when we would have time together. You never knew from one day to the next when or if Colin would be working and if he was working a 12 hour shift he would come home exhausted and be expected to be in early to do the same the following day. The casual work practices on the docks were causing huge stresses and strains for the entire family and so I felt that this dispute has not just been about work but about the company's attitude to the men and their families - they don't have the right to ruin our lives in the way they tried to after 1992.*

*I joined WOW at the first meeting on the 18 October 1995. The first two weeks of the dispute I was desperate to do something, I was so angry at MDHC. I wanted to go on the picket lines but Colin said there weren't any other women there, then he told me about the first WOW meeting and I went and became an active WOW member. Now I'm the deputy secretary of the group and fully involved in all our activities. I'm on the picket lines most mornings; I've been on the pickets to the houses of scabs and MDHC managers; I've been on delegations up and down the country to, among other places, Oxford, Leeds, Hull, Manchester, Nottingham, and Huddersfield; I handed our petition in to Downing Street and I've been to Paris.*

*The dispute has changed me dramatically. Before I think I was very emotional, I still am but I'm now much stronger and more confident. Before I was content being a mother and a housewife but now I want to go out into the world, I think I've found myself again and when the dispute finishes I want to stay politically active and get a job. There has also been changes in Colin's and my relationship. Before we were very traditional - he went out to work and earned the money and I took charge of the house and housekeeping. Now this has changed. Colin is much more involved at home - he has to be because I'm away so much. He takes the budget, cooks meals and looks after the house. Now we share roles and are both very supportive of each others union, political and outside activities.*

The women of WOW had no significant organised contact with each other before the dispute. Nevertheless, they quickly formed a unity of purpose and action which revealed a clarity of understanding regarding the wider issues associated with the dispute. In part, this reflects their immediate experience of the familial effects of casualisation but this is often also combined with the fact that many of the women originate from within the dock community and, as such, they possess, just as much as the men, the 'collective memory' of the history of life on the docks and the consequences of the poor working conditions that had once prevailed. These have been important in creating the group as an independent and powerful element within the dispute. The women have sent delegations to support other workers in struggle in various parts of the country, have played an important role in the organisation of the dockers' international conference, and have been invited to Sweden, Germany, France and Denmark to represent the dispute to women's groups and unions. The process of struggle has clearly altered, at least temporarily, the relationship between men and women in the dock community.

WOW was formed in October 1995. Doreen McNally, who is credited with starting the group, spoke at one of the early mass meetings and her description of the way in which her family life had been destroyed struck a chord with other women at the meeting. What they heard reflected their own lives and this was the spark that led the women to organise themselves formally into WOW. This is reflected in the range of comments made by WOW members describing why they joined the group. Jeanette joined:

> to show the MDHC that they were dealing with families not just the men and to meet other wives in the same situation as myself.

Val wished:

> to fight to get the sacked dockers their jobs back.

Cathy joined:

> because of the unfairness of my husband's dismissal after giving 34 years of loyal service - he certainly didn't deserve to be treated this way.

Dorothy reflects the views of many when she states:

> my husband and son had been sacked so I decided I must get involved because it was affecting me and my family for the future.

While Antoinette's reasons reflect a combination of family ties, family history and general political commitment:

47

## *Joan Bennett*

*I was born and brought up in Liverpool. My father was a docker. My husband's family have been on the docks for generations, both his father and grandfather worked there. His grandmother, Catherine Bennett, was one of the first women to work on the docks during the First World War. Along with six other women with whom she worked, she went to the Alexandra Dock when she heard that they were recruiting dockers and asked for work. Although her employment only lasted a few months, she was, nevertheless, a pioneer.*

*I became involved in WOW because I was so angry and disgusted at what they had done to my husband. After almost a quarter of a century of hard work we could lose everything. When the P45 came through the door it was a horrible feeling. The employers seemed to think that they could get away with anything. The mutual support I get from the Women of the Waterfront is really important. The men have meetings and they can have a pint and let it all out. When you are with others who understand it makes things a little easier. It does you good to come to the meetings where everyone understands we all have the same problems. If you are sitting in the house you just make yourself worse. I think this has done wonders for me. Sometimes there aren't enough hours in the day. Forget about the cleaning and housework that's not important anymore, this is the number one issue.*

*I have never been involved in anything like this before. I am the treasurer of WOW. The whole experience has boosted my confidence. We are all finding things in us we didn't know were there. I was a shy and quiet person before who would never have dreamed of speaking at meetings, now I feel quite confident about it. I was interested in politics before but didn't really give voice to my opinions, this experience has opened my horizons and made me realise that what is happening to us is happening to other working people. When we win I can't think of just going back to my life. Someone joked that we will have to look for other workers' struggles to support and maybe we will!*

My main reason was to support my sister and brother-in-law, but also I feel attached to the port through my family history. The dockers' campaign is also important to every working class person not just in Liverpool but world-wide.

Work, home and family commitments have meant that individuals have been involved in different ways depending on their own personal circumstances; some regularly attend meetings and events while others go to marches and pickets when they can. Nevertheless, WOW has established a clear role for itself in the dispute and has mobilised a large number of women to a range of activities.

The Women's group had the support of the Stewards' Committee from the beginning. As Jimmy Nolan notes:

I already knew about the tremendous role that women had played in the Miners' Strike and other struggles in this country....when one looks at the women now they have made a tremendous contribution to our struggle.

Mike Carden believes that:

The women have been like a hurricane of fresh air blowing through the dockers' movement and the TGWU......the women have shown tremendous skills and intelligence as the dispute has unfolded.

However, traditionally the dock industry in Britain has been a male dominated one and the workforce has had to change to accept the role of WOW in the dispute. This has been a significant change for many of the men. As Tony Nelson explains:

Other countries have women dockers and there would have been women on the strike committee. This is a white male dominated industry, over the last twenty years the men have never worked with any women or ethnic minorities and they had got to get over those prejudices....People have changed during this dispute; it has changed them and their old views and prejudices.

The comments of Billy Jenkins illustrate this process of change:

Personally, at first I wasn't too keen on the idea [of there being an active women's group] and I was a bit apprehensive, but that soon disappeared. Looking back on the dispute the women have been vitally important to us and every contribution they have made has been tremendous. ..Prior to the dispute I suppose I would be what you call an old fashioned male chauvinist through my own father. I always thought that the place for women was in the home, looking after the kids, which is a hard enough job. But you only have to look at the reactions of the others, for example, at the International Conferences, the first thing that the delegates have done is to enquire after WOW and the journalists that is the first thing they ask about. So obviously there is going to be a need for the women to organise themselves and get out of the kitchen.

Sixty women attended the first meeting of the women's group at Transport House. The women themselves acknowledge that initially they were unsure of exactly how to proceed and they looked to others for guidance. Two women Sylvia Pye and Aggi who had been active in the Women's Support Groups during the miners strike of 1984/5 came to the group and gave them some advice and, as a result, they established a committee to co-ordinate their activities.

WOW has access to the stewards' facilities at Transport House as well as having their own office there. The group has a weekly meeting in which the committee reports back on what has been happening, ensuring that all members are part of the decision-making process. Activities and delegation work are organised at the meetings and a steward attends to keep the women informed of the latest developments in the dispute. They also produce a monthly newsletter so that the women who cannot attend the meetings are kept fully informed of their activities. The newsletter is also given to the men at the mass meetings and is sent to the network of support groups throughout the country.

A number of the women always attend the weekly mass meetings and a report back by WOW is now a standing agenda item. Tony Nelson emphasises the significance of this:

> You have to understand that at the end of a mass meeting when you have Doreen McNally speaking, that would not have been heard of 10 years ago. It would not have happened.

Clearly WOW has developed an important and distinctive role for itself in the struggle against the MDHC, and has gained respect from the dockers as a consequence of its activities.

Although the women represent a range of experiences with regard to employment, union activity and political involvement, the majority of them has never been involved in an industrial dispute in this way and to this extent before. Initially their main activities included collecting money, attending the demonstrations and organising events for the dockers and their children. In some senses these activities could still be seen to reflect

# *Pat Walker*

*My husband has been a docker for 27 years and we have been married for 20. I currently work part-time in a small shop where there is no union. Obviously there has been disputes on the docks before but this is the first time there has ever been a women's support group. The way in which the men have been treated and the way in which the new contracts and conditions affected our families made this dispute different. There is a real feeling of injustice, this was an attack on our entire families and so it isn't about money, it's about jobs: my husband is only 43 he wants his job back but he has the right to work in decent conditions, to have set hours and to have time to spend at home.*

*I was involved in the group from the beginning, I couldn't have stayed at home, I wanted to know what was going on and to be involved. My children have been with me as well - on the marches and picket lines and they recognise how important the dispute is to all our lives. Many of the women had never met before, yet now there is a real sense of friendship and support. I think the women's group has been very important in maintaining the strike. We travel around the country with the men going to meetings and rallies. We received a tape from some of the women involved in the miners' strike and the parallels with how they organised are very clear. We have been involved in lots of activities, including bucket collections, delegation visits and picketing. The first time the women closed one of the dock gates we got a huge round of applause from the men but now they expect it of us and most of the men are very positive about our involvement. One of the more unusual things the women have done is go to houses of scabs and MDHC managers and sing our adopted song 'Big River'. While we are there we leaflet the surrounding area and houses informing people of our plight and making scabs known to their neighbours. We want to show the managers and the scabs that we fully support the men. The scabs don't think they have done anything wrong, but if they weren't in there, doing our men's jobs the dispute would be over by now.*

*At first the police were alright with the women, but as the dispute has gone on they have become more heavy handed, especially those from the Operational Services Division. A number of women on picket duty have been assaulted now by police officers. There is now a great feeling of solidarity between the men and women of the dock community and a feeling that together we can win.*

## *Irene Campbell*

*The port of Liverpool has played a significant part in my life. I was born in Liverpool in 1942 one of eight children. My father was a docker and we grew up in the dock area. My husband has been on the docks since 1966. His brother also worked in the port and his father was killed on the docks leaving his mother with five children to bring up.*

*I worked for British American Tobacco for 27 years. I was a shop steward in what was then the tobacco workers' union for almost twenty years. I wasn't very outspoken but I liked to get things done. Sometimes stewards would go in and talk 'official'. I liked to go to managers and get down to grass roots. When a girl was sacked for being late I went into the manager's office and said " Now listen, you can't sack her for being late a few times she has a young family at home. I'll get her up." We did that on a few occasions. We had a good relationship with the managers at BAT. Obviously you had official meetings but you could have good discussions with people even the managers had a heart. Clearly the MDHC managers don't!*

*Seven years ago the factory was threatened with closure and the whole workforce was to be made redundant. I was one of five women and seven men who staged a week long sit-in at the factory. These actions were very successful. Although the workforce was cut down the factory did not close but remained open for another six years. After the strike certain jobs were changed and for the first time women were allowed to be machine mechanics. This had previously been seen as a man's job. I felt this was also a victory for women as workers. I was one of eight women in the Liverpool factory who became a machine mechanic.*

*I became involved in the Women of the Waterfront by responding to Doreen McNally's invitation to get together. On the first meeting sixty women turned up. Although the circumstances are not those I would have chosen I have enjoyed working with all the other women. We are all good friends now. There is a lot of humour in this dispute from both the men and the women you couldn't get through this situation without it.*

*My husband is coming up sixty and had planned to retire next year. He could have taken the £25,000 and his pension but he wanted to stand by the other men who are younger and have children at home. At the beginning of the dispute the MDHC offered 200 men contracts mainly to younger men but they refused to take them and supported the older men and we should stand by them now. We have got to win this strike not just for ourselves but for the whole of the industry.*

women's traditional roles, the perpetuation of a supporting, family-centred role. However gradually, during the process of the dispute, WOW has taken an increasingly active, public and campaigning role; for example, they have been to Downing Street to present a petition to John Major demanding that he intervene[38] and more recently they wrote to Bill Morris asking why hardship payments had not been made (see chapter 4). The changing role of WOW has been acknowledged by the stewards, as Bobby Morton has commented:

> The stewards' initial thoughts were that the women could take some of the weight off us...they had not been politically educated and, without being disrespectful, they were purely housewives who went about their normal business. They have developed from there and 13 months later you couldn't find a group of women who are more politically and industrially aware than WOW. They have developed so much it's incredible...They have gained their own identity now and are so much more than a support group.

While Jimmy Nolan argues:

> In the beginning the women had to find their own way and we didn't interfere...It is better that they developed their own consciousness... and when one sees them now it is clear that they have advanced very rapidly.

One of the more original and interesting tactics developed by WOW has been to picket the houses of both the directors and senior managers of MDHC as well as those of local Liverpool scabs. Their purpose was to expose the complacency and contempt shown by MDHC managers and scabs towards the dock families. This activity first occurred in December 1995 when the women and their children sang Christmas carols to the occupants, but as Christmas passed, they adopted the song 'Big River' by Jimmy Nail as their anthem. While 'entertaining' the scabs they post leaflets through their doors and those of their neighbours, pointing out that they are stealing dockers jobs and that they should respect the picket lines.

As Christmas passed and it became clear the dispute was likely to last some time, WOW's activities began to expand. The confidence of the women in taking on these new roles was also growing and they became involved in all aspects of the dispute. From having an important, though secondary and supportive, role they have established themselves as an important and leading section of the dispute. Again this has been recognised by the stewards. Tony Nelson comments:

They are different from other support groups and they have told us that on numerous occasions. They are different because they are involved in the families and they need to be treated differently.

Mike Carden adds:

WOW has to be closer than any other support group because they are the wives and partners of the Liverpool dockers and they have got to have recognition and respect because of that.

As with the Strike Committee, running WOW and participating in its activities has become a seven day a week occupation for its members. As Irene comments:

I am never at home, my life has changed completely. I don't know how I found the time to do a full-time job before. I have become a picket line name. Dockers have always had nicknames most probably they have now given nicknames to all the WOW.

As the activities of WOW have expanded and changed so have the roles and expectations of the women involved. Collective action, within WOW and between WOW and the dockers has created a bond of solidarity which has, in turn, increased their confidence to do more and take on 'non-traditional' roles. As Cathy says, she has been amazed to watch:

members within the group finding an inner strength they never knew they had. The solidarity of the members the courage and care shown to each other.

Antoinette notes similar themes:

the biggest impact has been the camaraderie, friendship, solidarity and spirit of all involved in the WOW, their determination is an inspiration.

While Jeanette notes the:

comradeship and pulling together and the knowledge that what we are doing has worth. We cannot be ignored we are an organisation in our own right.

For Margaret the conclusions have also been more general:

The comradeship and togetherness and supporting each other has made me more aware of what is happening to the working class in this country.

While Doreen has also been affected by the solidarity received from outside the dock community:

The solidarity and support of working people around the country has been marvellous. [But equally important is] how we have all pulled together, all of us with our different responsibilities and personalities.

The women have become increasingly involved in activities which were initially seen to be the domain of the men. They are now a constant presence on the picket line, not only joining with the men on the mass pickets but also being an effective force on their own: WOW regularly cover gates on their own during the day and at the mass pickets, and the women have closed the gates on numerous occasions. They have also increased their involvement by speaking at meetings, locally, nationally and internationally, as well as doing radio and television interviews. As Dorothy argues:

> we spread the word on how the dispute is progressing to the four corners of the country to any organisations who want to know and help. As the dispute progressed so did WOW. We have our own banner which takes a proud place in all the marches and rallies home and away. We have our own badge. I think we are an important cog in getting the dispute known about despite the media blackout.

Jeanette makes similar points:

> The role has changed from a voice in the background to a more powerful voice alongside our men. We are the ones who cope on a day to day basis with home, children, our own jobs, plus giving physical and moral support to our men who stand on the picket lines each day watching scabs drive by to do their work...It's been a long haul but with our support and the support from workers world-wide our men will go back to work.

While Antoinette reflects on how much the group has grown:

> The moral support and encouragement has evolved into physical support in the sense that the WOW are participating as main speakers at the national and international conferences, [we also have] women only marches, rallies and pickets. In effect we are playing a greater part in the dispute than ever envisaged by all involved including ourselves.

As Joan sums it up: "we have gone from the kitchen sink to addressing conferences".

The women have also gone on international delegations to attend conferences and meetings in Sweden, Holland, Denmark, Germany and France. While on their trip to Sweden Colette and Mary were asked to speak at a rally for International Women's Day. As Colette recalls:

> it was a rally for International Women's Day , they felt their women needed a push. They were impressed by our women with their involvement in the dispute and they thought it may help to create more unity between the men and women in the union.....I told of what the women were doing, their involvement, the scabs and the vigils the women hold. [I told them] how we close Seaforth gates and generally how the women who have never done anything like this before have got up and proved themselves to be worthy and capable of doing a good job."[39]

The ability of the women to be such effective ambassadors for the dispute stems from the fact that they have an intimate knowledge of the way in which the changing nature of dock work is altering the nature of family life. Also, in common with the men and as a result of the dynamic of the dispute, the women have developed a wider political perspective on the dispute's causes. Irene states:

> The sackings were engineered by MDHC. If it had not been the Torside men's sacking it would have been something else, this has been brewing for a long time.

For Joan:

> [Introducing] casual labour, trying to get rid of the trade unions and organised labour, that is the number one issue for the MDHC.

For Mary, those causes must be addressed in any settlement:

> Every man must be re-employed with better working conditions and hours so they are able to work without becoming so stressed.

While Christine's conclusions are more general. She states that the problem is:

> Profits taking precedence over human needs (with) greedy bosses stripping the rights from workers supported by the capitalist government.

The changing role of WOW and its importance to the dispute over such a long period has been acknowledged by both the strike committee and the men themselves and clearly challenges traditional gender roles within the community: it challenges the previous assumptions of the men as some

## *Cathy Dwyer*

*I am from Liverpool and my father was a seafarer. We always lived by the docks when I was growing up. Andy has been on the docks for 34 years. The way the men were treated was disgraceful. They were dismissed for standing by their morals and principals. They were not sacked for stealing or misconduct but for holding to the principle of never crossing a picket line. WOW is important because we all need to pull togther to support one another. I thought we would get together and help each other out by sharing groceries and talking. I never imagined that we would become so deeply involved in the dispute.*

*I have been on the picket line everyday and have been on delegation work. The first time I went to a union conference in Blackpool they told us that we were going to address a fringe meeting. I didn't even know what that was! I have picketed scab's and director's houses and attended all the marches and rallies. I have been down the picket line every day. At first I think some of the men didn't think we should be there. But the first time the women and children shut down the gate, which was a historic event and felt wonderful, the men who had been on another gate marched down to where we were and stood and applauded us. It was one of my proudest moments.*

*The dock board planned this dispute but they hadn't thought it through and they underestimated the courage of the men. When the first International Conference took place I remember looking at all the dockers with great admiration for actually organising such an event, I was very proud of them. After 12 months I am still proud of them for fighting for what is theirs.*

of the comments of the partners of WOW activists demonstrate. Charlie McNally observes:

> Now I ask her about what is going on in the dispute. I do a lot more around the house. She is out more than I am on delegation work.

Keith Walker reflects on his new skills around the house:

> I'd never been in the kitchen before......I can use a can opener now! I make the beds and hoover during the week, not just at the weekends.

Equally the men have noticed the way the women themselves have changed. As Keith says:

> Pat has changed...she has more interest and understanding of social issues outside our family.... Sometimes I get dispirited with picketing everyday and it's Pat who encourages me who gets up at 5am to go to the picket and says 'come on you can do this'.

Jimmy Campbell notes:

> When the women get up and speak they don't gloss over things the way some other people do.

The dispute, and their activities within it, has also altered the women's perceptions of themselves, their roles and their 'world outlook'. For some of the women these are political and personal changes which they did not expect.

Cathy states:

> It has taught me to speak up more for myself and not to allow any person you come across in life to treat you badly.

For Margaret:

> It has made me a stronger person in mind and body.

Joan says:

> if anyone would have told me that I would be addressing meetings all over the country I would have said "not me" but you have so much anger at what they have done that you just don't think about it. You just want to tell people the truth.

While, more reflectively, Pat argues:

> It has awakened my awareness of the treatment of workers by greedy bosses. I was just a housewife and mother before but I can see further than my home to things that are going on all around the country to the workers and their families.

The changing nature of how the women see themselves and their role has obvious parallels with Women's Support Groups in the Miners' Strike of 1984/5. The changes that the women have experienced both politically and personally have been a revelation to many of them: their involvement in the dispute has given them the confidence to express their views publicly and move beyond the expectations of both themselves and others with regard to the role they had to play in this struggle. WOW not only attends rallies, marches and conferences as representatives of the dispute but are now asked independently, by other groups of workers, to join with them in their struggles. In particular, close links of solidarity have developed between WOW and striking women from the Hillingdon hospital in London. For the women, the purpose of WOW is to work alongside the men to win this dispute but it is also clear that, for many of them, their involvement in the dispute has brought about a dramatic change in their view of the world and the roles and activities they now expect to play.

However, the parallels with the Women's Support Groups in the Miners' Strike are not exact. The dispute is much smaller and far more isolated than was the case in the 1984/85 struggle. The general level of confrontation between workers, employers and the state has been less intense and there has been far less generalised support from a range of groups in society. These features have set partial limits on what has occurred. Although WOW is capable of mobilising significant numbers of women for its activities, such as the family pickets, the activists who regularly attend the meetings and are involved in delegation work represent a minority of the dockers' wives, partners and families. In addition, it is only within the ranks of these activists that we see the most substantial changes in peoples' lives. Nevertheless, the activities of WOW and the changes that have occurred are an important example of the developments that can and do affect people when they become involved in political struggles and industrial disputes. It is an example of how people's attitudes, values and political consciousness changes, often very rapidly, during periods of intense social upheaval. Whether these changes will have lasting effects on these women beyond this dispute is yet to be determined. However, they are already talking of continuing the group beyond this particular battle, not only to maintain contact with one another but to offer support to other workers in struggle which would indicate that at least some of these changes are here to stay.

*WOW and their children leafleting and singing outside scabs houses, December 1995.*

*WOW show an MDHC director their support for the men by visiting his home.*

*Cathy Dwyer and Irene Campbell with WOW'S first banner.*

*Six months into the dispute and WOW has established its prominent role including having their own banner on rallies (March 1996)*

*(Left)*
*Sue Mitchell*
*reporting to the*
*mass meeting*
*on behalf of*
*WOW.*

*(Below)*
*Women from WOW and*
*their children on the*
*Community Rally ,*
*19ᵗʰ August 1996.*

*The WOW float at the Anniversary Rally, 28ᵗʰ September 1996.*

*Joan Bennett on the WOW float at the
Anniversary Rally, 28ᵗʰ September 1996.*

63

*(Left)*
*Doreen Mc Nally*
*addresses the*
*Anniversary Rally,*
*28th September 1996*

*(Below)*
*The women join the*
*international*
*campaign. Colette*
*and Mary on their*
*way to Sweden to*
*represent the dockers*
*at a series of meetings*
*and rallies.*

*22 November 1995*

## *TO WIVES, PARTNERS, SISTERS AND DAUGHTERS*

*We are the Liverpool Dockers' support group, known as "Women of the Waterfront." We, like you, are close to someone who has been treated disgracefully by M.D.H.C.*

*With the men, we believe that every man must be reinstated. This will only happen if we all work together to help to widen support for our cause and support the men in a positive way.*

*The vast majority of us have never before belonged to an organised group of this nature; even those of us who are committee members. Most of us have led our lives on the sidelines; bringing up our families and holding down our own jobs. Our men, and probably yours, were happy for us to remain away from "the action" while they, with the help of the stewards, fought for reinstatement. They were too proud to ask for help.*

*However, we saw the need to face facts: that we must all play our part to end this awful situation. M.D.H.C. Directors have shown a callousness without precedent. They seem to have a disregard for human dignity and suffering unless it is their own.*

*A very few men deserted us at the beginning and they will have to live with their consciences for the rest of their lives.*

*There is now rock-solid support for our cause. Some of us have managed to go outside of Merseyside to meet with sympathetic and influential groups and have been amazed and humbled to find the esteem in which Liverpool dockers are held.*

*What you read in the press does not even begin to give an idea of where that support is and how great its magnitude. The stewards are working incredibly hard on the national and international fronts and many more people are working tirelessly to organise events to raise funds for those families most affected by the situation.*

*This is where your help, however small, would be much appreciated. Please come along to our next Wednesday evening meeting (7.00 p.m. start) in Transport House, where a creche is available, if required. A list of committee members is enclosed should you wish to speak to someone first.*

*We firmly believe that we will win this fight because morality and human decency are on our side. Victory will come all the sooner if you demonstrate that you are too.*

*With Regards from the "WOMEN OF THE WATERFRONT."*

# Chapter 4

## Lock Out on the Liverpool Waterfront

As we outlined in the introduction, the lock-out on the docks was manufactured in the last week of September 1995. Once the dockers had been sacked and locked out the dispute gradually crystallised into its current struggle. Many of the dockers are convinced that MDHC thought they would disappear and the matter would be over quickly. However, Liverpool remains a city with severe unemployment and it is clear that many of the dockers would be unlikely to find work again. In these circumstances, the tradition of organisation, the lack of alternatives and full familial support combined to create a very powerful opponent to MDHC's strategy and it is clear they underestimated the willingness of the workers and their families to fight for their jobs.

Over the last twelve months the dispute has developed in a number of different ways. With the exception of the most bureaucratically organised and controlled disputes, industrial confrontations are not 'wars of position', static stand-offs between managers and workers, rather they are events in which new initiatives and practices are constantly brought to the fore as each side develops new tactics in an attempt to achieve their victory. In this atmosphere, outside support and initiatives are often crucial to bolster the sides in any dispute. MDHC has been influenced by the support it has received from the government, from local businesses organised through the Chamber of Commerce, from local right-wing supporters who appeared in press advertisements attacking the workforce, praising MDHC and, *de facto*, supporting casualisation and cheapening jobs throughout Merseyside;[40] and from anti-union firms like the Canadian line CAST. The activities of these 'outside agitators' have clearly influenced MDHC's conduct during the dispute.

## Terry Southers

*My father was a docker as are my brothers, they all went to sea before working on the docks and I followed this pattern. At the age of 16 I went into the merchant navy. I was at sea for 9 years before I 'came ashore' in 1971 and got a job with the Mersey Docks Board as a fitter's labourer. In 1973 there was an intake of dockers and my brothers got me on via the 'deceased members priority' (my father had died the year before and I got his job). I was employed by the National Dock Labour Board and was sent to work in Liverpool Maritime Terminals. They put you through a kind of apprenticeship, training you on different aspects of the job. Eventually I became a member of a 'puddling gang' working with various oils, discharging the oil and then cleaning the tanks - this was a fairly specialised work so I was permanently in the holds. In 1981 I hurt my shoulder and was unable to do the necessary climbing around the tanks so I became a deckhand. Later that year the firm went into liquidation so I went into the 'sin bin' waiting to be placed in another yard, I got sent to Liverpool stevedoring but this only lasted a year before I got placed with 'Coastal' where I was a gantry driver until the present dispute broke out.*

*Prior to 1989 it was a pleasure to work on the docks but after abolition it just became another job. The atmosphere changed and our conditions of work were gradually eroded. In 1991 I was put on a probationary year because I was involved in supporting the events at the Pandoro ferry. I've always been an activist. I joined miners' pickets in 1984/85 and travelled up and down the country in the 1989 strike against abolition of the NDLS, but I only became a steward 6 months before the present dispute. I've always thought that every man should be a steward - that we should all be prepared to stand up for ourselves against the bosses.*

*At the start of this dispute we were faced with two choices: to scab or not to scab - the majority of Liverpool dockers showed that they were not scabs. My father and brothers fought the hard fight to get decent work conditions and union recognition. We have to fight now to maintain their victories.*

On the dockers' side, the present struggle has gone through a number of distinct phases, developing in response to the interaction of four influences. First, the relative successes and failures of their campaign. Tactics have been evaluated throughout the dispute with the result that some have been dropped, others modified and others given greater prominence. These tactics have been judged in light of the ideas dominant within the dispute and these ideas are the outcome of an interaction with, and conflict between, two sources: the dominant political ideas within the shop stewards' committee and the influence of supporters from outside the docks; these represent the next two influences on how the dispute has been run. The first of these are the expectations and the political ideologies of the dispute's leadership. Leadership of the campaign rests with the powerful shop stewards' strike committee, which contains a number of individuals who are experienced political and union activists. They have had a crucial influence on the shape of the campaign. The dominant beliefs within the shop stewards' committee, as publicly expressed at mass meetings, are: that industrial relations law has effectively shackled the trade unions; that the TGWU leadership are doing everything within their means to support the dockers; that after 17 years of Conservative governments, the British working class has been significantly weakened and is unable to deliver industrial solidarity; that it is impossible to ask workers in other industries for support without first going through their own union machinery, and that, given the legal situation and the weakness of trade unionism in Britain, it is essential to look to other sources of support in order to win the dispute. Whether, or to what extent, any of these beliefs is accurate is less important than the *fact* that they represent the political perspectives of the dockers' leadership and they have had a real effect in shaping the conduct of the dispute. Of course, it is not the case that all the stewards accept all of these contentions. There are clear differences between the stewards, but their adherence to a policy of 'collective responsibility' has meant that each steward is tied to the dominant, majority opinion within the leadership. Finally, although these are the dominant ideas within the leadership of the dispute, they are not completely monolithic. There has been times when there has been friction between the stewards, between the stewards and the dockers, between the stewards and outside supporters and between the stewards and the TGWU officials.

The campaign has also developed in response to ideas, actions and debates initiated from either dockers themselves or by outside activists and supporters who identify with the campaign for re-instatement. In the early months of the campaign, for example, regular Saturday meetings

## *Billy Jenkins*

*When I left school I went to sea for 5 years before going on the docks in 1969. My dad was a docker as were both my brothers. From 1969 up until 1989 I worked as a holdsman. I worked on loads of different ships and cargoes. The work was often dirty and very hard but I enjoyed it, there was always a great atmosphere and great camaraderie between the men you'd work with. Health and safety issues and work and pay conditions weren't bad and if there was a problem the stewards could always sort it out. Things changed after 1989. The camaraderie went a bit, the bosses attitudes changed and became more aggressive and safety went out the window. Safety was always our main thing - a job had to be safe- but after 1989 if there was a job we thought wasn't right, the supervisor and boss would come and they'd send for the safety officer (who was employed by MDHC) and he'd always give it the go ahead, everything we said wasn't safe he just gave the nod to. The supervisors' attitudes was "you got a job, what more do you want" and the officer of the union - he was no different to the boss, he'd say "its changed now boys, you're lucky to have a job, look at the other ports". This dispute is so important. We've got to end casualisation, improve working conditiaons and get safety back on the agenda. We are due some respect because we have built this industry (and rebuilt Liverpool port since 1989 to make it profitable again). And we've got to get the union right, so that it represents us and has decent full-time officials elected by us and accountable to us - we are thwe union.*

were held with shop stewards from across the city.[41] In making this point it is important to emphasise that we are not suggesting the dispute has been taken over or 'unduly influenced' by political activists. Rather, that for those involved, industrial disputes tend to offer new experiences, challenge old practices and ways of thinking and, hence offer a forum where a variety of ideas, activities and practices will be openly debated, no matter what their origin, so long as they are generally supportive of the campaign being waged. In these circumstances a wider dialogue can open up between participants and supporters over appropriate tactics. Thus, disputes can be seen as a process in which political ideas, in their widest sense, will shape the tactics being followed. The consequence of this dialogue during the present lock-out has been to maintain a level of dynamism throughout the last twelve months, which has in turn kept both the confidence and the participation levels of dockers, relatively high. The final factor affecting the dockers' campaign has been the influence of the official trade union movement, especially the TGWU. The relationship between the dockers, their stewards and the TGWU officials has often been fraught. As we noted, defence of the TGWU's position has been a key element shaping the stewards thinking, so, on the one hand, dockers have been informed at mass meetings that the national officials have been a great help and have been doing everything behind the scenes to promote the dockers' cause [see, for example, Mass Meetings on 1 March 1996; 3 April 1996, 19 April 1996, 19 July 1996]. The stewards, although running an unofficial dispute, have operated out of Transport House. The TGWU National Docks Officer, Jack Adams, has been in regular contact with the stewards and has been involved in negotiations with MDHC (on occasions without any dock stewards being present). And Bill Morris was praised by stewards for attending a mass meeting of dock workers on Wednesday 13 March 1996. At that meeting he told the assembled workers and supporters that:

> It is one of those situations that as you age and your grandchildren say to you 'where were you at the great moment', you either stand up with pride and say 'I was there' or you hang your head in shame without an answer. I tell you this, when my grandchildren say to me in 15, 20 or 25 years from now, where were you when the Liverpool dockers were fighting for their jobs, their dignity, their community and their pride, I want to be able to say 'I was there marching with them side by side until they got their jobs back'...This is not going to be a short-term victory...It is going to be a victory for every docker in the world - because Liverpool dockers will never walk alone.

Unlike many unofficial disputes,[42] the TGWU national officials have offered the dockers verbal support and the use of the union premises and machinery for negotiations, elements which highlight the continuing link between the stewards and the union officials.

On the other hand, the lack of practical and (limited) financial support from the TGWU has been heavily criticised by dock workers in the open sessions in a number of mass meetings [see, for example, Mass Meetings on 26 April 1996; 10 May 1996; 6 Sept 1996]. The failure of TGWU port officials to deliver physical support during the dispute has also been attacked by stewards [Mass Meeting 26 July 1996] and dockers at the open session [see, for example, Mass Meeting 26 April 1996; 10 May 1996, 6 September 1996]. The stewards have also expressed frustration at being denied access to the TGWU hardship funds to which they and their members have contributed over a number of years [Mass Meetings 19 & 26 July 1996; 6 Sept 1996]. Bill Morris at the meeting on the 13 March 1996 told the dockers:

> I am here to re-affirm the executive council's commitment and support, I am here to speak on behalf of the union, I am here to say to you that, whatever happens, our spirit will never be broken and our bellies will never be starved ...

Such fine statements have not been matched in reality. As Val said:

> Bill Morris cares more about his funds than his members. They are rolling in money and they are not giving any to us. The TGWU leaders are terrified of the Tories...We've had to battle for our funds...The dockers have paid their union dues for 20 to 40 years. Morris should remember who's paying his wages.[43]

By 26 July 1996 the stewards were clearly frustrated about receiving limited money from the hardship funds. Jimmy Davies told the mass meeting:

> We indicated our displeasure with the TGWU...[and the situation]...with the hardship payments...is absolutely disgraceful. We said [to the union] that money is ours and we are no longer going to be begging for it, we are telling you that we want it...we are not going to stand by and see lads who have served thirty odd years on the docks facing repossession of their houses. We are not going to allow anybody...to lose property. We said to [the union]...to start getting the hardship payments through to us on a regular basis and if you don't we'll have to take action ourselves...It's absolutely appalling what is going with the T&G.

**T&G**

CENTRAL OFFICE

Transport House  Palace Street  Victoria  London  SW1E 5JD
Telephone: (0171) 828 7788  Facsimile: (0171) 630 5861

BM/SAW/GJ

5 August 1996
[Dictated by Bill Morris and
signed in his absence]

Dear

Thank you for your letter of the 25th July.

Let me say at the outset that I resent any suggestion that the Union is giving less than one hundred per cent support to the dismissed dockers. Whilst we are making every effort to find a negotiated settlement and to relieve hardship being experienced by our membership, this is not an official dispute and it would therefore be inappropriate for the Union's machinery to be used to promote it. To do otherwise would jeopardise the limited assistance we are currently able to give.

Nevertheless, the union **has** supported the Families' Hardship Fund and has engaged the Union's solicitors to take industrial tribunal cases in respect of those who have a case for unfair dismissal given that there were on holiday, or sick etc., at the time the dispute began.

Quite apart from that sort of practical help, I led negotiations to a point where MDHC made an offer of a figure which the Executive Officers described, at the time, as being the best possible; that remains our view. The Deputy General Secretary, Jack Adams, continues negotiations with the company and we shall continue to do whatever is possible to give support to the dockers and their families and to seek a resolution of the dispute.

Yours sincerely,

*Bill Morris*

**BILL MORRIS**
General Secretary
*pp smutclsn*

(Photostat 2)
*TGWU letter*

**Strike** bulletin

Written by supporters of *Socialist Worker*

# We can win... but not like this!

The gloves are off in our strike and the bosses are serious about beating us. They have called in the union busters Drake Port Services who have a record of introducing casual labour in Tilbury and in Southampton 3 years ago they recruited scabs. The bosses have a strategy to beat us but our strategy now is not going to beat them.

There are 2 approaches in this strike. The one that dominates now relies on public opinion and the goodwill of councillors, MPs and the clergy to get our jobs back. The other welcomes such support but mobilises the real strength in support of us - that is workers in Liverpool and around the country whose solidarity can ensure we have money and mass pickets. It is time that this second strategy dominated our strike.

Organised workers have the power to win this strike. We have to mobilise that for its best use. The demonstrations we need are ones that march on the dock gate to stop the scabs.

Public sympathy is great but we need to break the Tories laws to win. We know the media and the police will be on the bosses side when the crunch comes but the workers we address now will side with us.

Bill Morris is not gunning for us and he is not going to back our strike. He is more frightened of the Tories laws than he is for the future of unions in Merseyside and beyond. Even the councillors who mouth sympathy are still watching MDHC take money from them.

Scabs are getting in. We have to close the port down to win. A call from us for a mass picket now to workers around the country would have them flooding up the dock road. That mass picket at the gate means the scabs have a hard time and we all get a boost from the support, while the bosses get a real taste of the numbers on our side.

We are not just fighting for ourselves. If we win, there will be a brake put on the bosses attacks in other workplaces. If we loose, the green light will be given to the bosses to beat the Firefighters and start to take on Fords and other workers.

We have to do now what it takes to win. There has to be official strike committee collection sheets and requests for solidarity in their thousands sent out to all workers. There has to be a date fixed for the mass picket and work done to build for it. Thats the way to beat the bosses.

**Read Socialist Worker, 50p weekly**

(Photostat 3)
*Supporters leaflet*

# Strike bulletin

Written by supporters of *Socialist Worker*

# Mass pickets - *The way to win.*

Saturday's demo proved to us all again how much support we have - but how can ⌄ we use it best to win our strike?

Workers don't just want to cheer us on from the sidelines, they want to stop the union busting bosses too.

They know as much as we do that the port has to stop working completely. We are wasting the chance to use that support to stop the scabs.

We are all frustrated at watching the scabs going in, knowing they are doing our work and that Drakes will be organising to get more in.

We need a mass picket - but what does that mean?

A mass picket is about putting a call out to workers in Liverpool and from around the country to join us in force to stop the scabs and that means blocking the road. Therefore we need to put out a date and time several days in advance so workers can build support, knowing what is asked of them. They will come because they want to see us win and they don't want bosses to have a victory to take on unions across Merseyside.

Of course this means taking on the bosses' laws to win. Every worker today faces the same problem and they will support us defying those laws because it is the only way we can win.

Of course the media will spread the bosses' lies but the real public opinion that matters is the workers who put the money in the bucket and join us on the picket line.

We are wasting that sympathy if we don't turn it into action.

Mass mobilisations have to make a difference to our strike winning. Lets use the thousands who marched for us round town to prevent those lorries and cars going through the gate. We have to go for this strategy now because every day we lose, the bosses use to their advantage.

The talks we waited for really took the piss, they insulted us with that offer and we told them to take a hike.

We shouldn't wait now for MPs and councillors to do more talking for us - lets take the fight and our supporters to the docks and shut it down.

## *Read Socialist Worker, 50p weekly*

(Photostat 3a)
*Supporters leaflet*

74

# Support The Dockers

## Join the
## *SOLIDARITY*
# *PICKET*

---

**Tuesday**
**19th December**
**6.00 am**
Seaforth Container Terminal
Bootle Docks

---

500 Dockers continue their fight against
casualisation and brutal sackings.
They need our continued support and solidarity.
Bring food, toys and any donations
to the picket line.

# STUFF THE BOSSES THIS CHRISTMAS

(Photostat 4)
*Mass Picket leaflet*

75

By late July 1996 the financial situation of many dockers was becoming desperate and WOW organised their members to write to Bill Morris asking for his help. The reply the women received started by informing the women he resented any insinuation that he was giving less than 100 per cent support and then proceeded to inform them it was an unofficial dispute so the union couldn't do more than the minimum. Finally, he argued that the offer of financial settlement that the union had obtained in February (see below) was the best that could be obtained. (see Photostat 2). Despite Bill Morris's indignation at the suggestion that he was not doing enough, Jimmy informed the Mass Meeting on 30 August 1996 that:

Once again it gives us no pleasure to tell you that, yet again, we have received no money from the TGWU.

By the end of September 1996, one year into the dispute, the dockers' hardship fund had received 9 payments of £30,000 from the TGWU, between the 500 dockers this amounted to £540 each for the year.

The growing unease and conflict with the TGWU is matched by antagonism to the inactivity of other union leaders. Some delegates to union conferences have voiced concern over their treatment by officials [Mass Meeting 3 May 1996], while there have been increasing demands from the stewards that the trade union leadership should provide solidarity action. As Jimmy Davies said at the Mass Meeting 27 September 1996:

It's time for trade union officials to stop sitting on the fence...we demand...support...[Over the years] Liverpool dockers have supported workers from up and down the country - we need their support now...and not just moral support we need physical support from our fellow trade unionists.

At the same meeting Jimmy Nolan argued:

union leaders should call and lead industrial action in support of dockers and against the law.

Thus the dispute has been marked by a growing tension between the leadership of the dispute and the trade union officials.

From the beginning, the dispute was organised through the strike committee which is made up of the members of the former shop stewards committee and other (non-elected) union activists. This group meet on a daily basis and it is at these meetings that the tactics of the dispute are formed and discussed. Mass meetings are held at least once a week and reports are presented to the workforce and debate and questions can be raised in this forum. The strike committee have near unanimous support for the way they have conducted the dispute and the ways they have developed their tactics. Initially the strategy followed by the strike committee was composed of two elements. First, as far as possible, the dockers should keep the dispute within the legal parameters established by Industrial Relations law. This was difficult in so far as the dockers had formally broken the law on 28 September when they refused to cross the Torside workforces' picket lines, but by the afternoon of Thursday 28 September, senior TGWU officials had met directors from MDHC who informed them that they would not be taking any legal action against the union. Despite the fact that on-going negotiations were taking place, that evening MDHC intensified matters by hiring a private security firm and couriers to hand-deliver redundancy notices to their direct dock employees. The following evening MDHC issued somewhere in the region of 180 'personal contracts' to some of their dock employees. These contracts make it clear that MDHC had decided to introduce fully casualised working practices and arrangements and that they had abandoned their strategy of recognising the TGWU, a tacit recognition that their strategy of union incorporation had failed. Despite this setback, the workforce, under union advice, attempted to return to work on 9 and 10 October 1995, only to be met by locked gates and police officers barring their way: the workforce had been locked out from their place of work.[44] As company spokesperson, Eric Leatherbarrow, brutally put it:

> There is no point in the men coming into work because they are no longer employees of Mersey Docks.[45]

Indeed MDHC asked Merseyside police to arrest workers entering the port gates on charges of trespassing.[46]

The second element of their strategy was to try and mobilise public opinion and the support of recognised community leaders, like MP's, councillors and the clergy.[47] The high point of this campaign was the first Community March and Rally held on 21 October 1995, which assembled and started at Liverpool's Roman Catholic Cathedral. An advert taken out in the Liverpool Echo (20 October 1995) lists the breadth of community support the dockers had obtained. The march was led by church leaders and local MP's and obtained substantial support from community and labour and trade union organisation across Merseyside. In this atmosphere, the Liverpool Echo, not noted for its radicalism, came out in support of re-instatement in its leader column. It argued:

> MDHC must heed growing opinion on Merseyside urging the reinstatement of the dockers.[48]

77

The build up of community pressure may have been partially responsible for the first 'Final offer' of settlement issued by MDHC on 18 October 1995. It applied only to former employees of MDHC and Coastal Containers Ltd, but offered nothing to employees of Nelson Freight or Torside. According to the Stewards the settlement contained three offers:

1. 150 jobs would be contracted to Drake Port Services. Sacked dock workers could apply for these posts, but 'no guarantee can be given that Drake will recruit former dockers only:'

2. The establishment of a co-operative composed of sacked Liverpool dockers but with 'no exclusive right being given to such an organisation:'

3. A lump sum ex-gratia payment of £10,000.[49]

As the stewards state:

> MDHC subsequently confirmed its intention to contract dockers' work to Drake Port Services on 20 October 1995...The offer of casual employment and severance was rejected at a subsequent mass meeting of sacked dock workers.[50]

The offer was clearly unacceptable to the workforce. However, the local press and some community leaders saw the offer as acceptable, or at least the basis for further negotiations and this seemed to indicate that there were certain limits to the public opinion/community focused campaign the dockers were undertaking: put bluntly within the 'community' there were many who were opposed to the re-instatement campaign or whose objective was to obtain some form of negotiated settlement between the dockers and MDHC which fell short of re-instatement. As October moved into November sections of the workforce were clearly growing impatient and demands for a more active strategy started to be raised. In particular two strike bulletins written by dockers who were supporters of the paper *Socialist Worker* argued for a strategy composed of, first, mass picketing to close the docks and obtain support from other workers in Liverpool and, secondly, for greater emphasis on delegation visits to factories and offices throughout the country to raise solidarity and force the dispute onto the national agenda. (see Photostats 3 and 3a).

Picketing has been an integral part of the dockers' campaign since the dispute started and virtually all the dockers have been involved in the picketing schedule. It is important to stress that one of the key factors in the ability of the dockers to maintain the dispute over such a long period is the generally high level of involvement amongst the sacked workforce, and the solidarity they have received from their families, communities and political activists in Liverpool. Thus, the picketing has maintained the pressure on the scab workforce and has severely disrupted the ability of the port to continue its daily business. But mass picketing, with the aim of closing the docks, was not initially part of the dockers' strategy. It may seem strange that such a traditional method of organising and winning disputes, had not been considered before but, as Tony, the shop steward with responsibility for this activity, argues: "we'd never had to do it before, strikes had always been solid". Further, of course, organising mass pickets meant breaking the law and initially the stewards, after seeking advice from the TGWU, wanted to avoid such a confrontation. The arguments presented within the bulletins were not immediately accepted by all the participants in the dispute, but they did start a debate over tactics. Eventually delegation work became much more systematically organised and is now (twelve months into the dispute) an integral feature of the dockers' campaign. Mass pickets by dockers were organised by mid-November. By December a hardship fund had been set up, with fund-raising activities being undertaken across Liverpool: the money was crucial to see the dockers and their families through the Christmas period and to build up national and international solidarity. In the pre-Christmas period supporters started to bring presents and gifts to the pickets lines and this was a major boost for morale at that time of year. Finally, by late November the dockers were calling for workers throughout Britain to support them on mass pickets of the dock gates. Notification of the times and place of pickets were set in advance and posted to supporters throughout the country. As a result a number of very significant 6 a.m. pickets of the Seaforth Container Terminal took place (see Photostat 4) and these led to the dock gates being shut, something which had not happened before.[51]

However, the tactic of calling mass pickets has been used sparingly during the dispute. The stewards have argued that it has two weaknesses. First, it allows MDHC and the shipping lines to make alternative arrangements for the days and times of the pickets. Secondly, it gives the police the opportunity to prepare and thus increases the chances of violent confrontation between dockers, their supporters and the police. Given the size and age profile of the dock workforce this is thought to be counter productive (although by July 1996 the police became a lot more aggressive in their methods and regularly started picking up those they considered 'ring leaders' on marches and pickets: the absence of mass pickets did not stop police harassment and confrontation between dockers and the police).

It also reflects the continuing hold of the idea of winning 'public opinion' to the dockers' cause: the stewards believe that scenes of violence from the picket line damage public support for workers in disputes. As a result the stewards have developed a 'hit and run' picketing tactic. Dockers are given a list, at each week's mass meeting, of the following week's picket roster, informing dockers when there will be 'normal' pickets and when there will be dockers' mass pickets. This tactic has allowed the dockers and the women's support group to take MDHC and the police by surprise and has led to dock gates being closed, with resultant delays on ships still using the port. But the tactic hinders other groups of workers from joining the dockers at the port gates.

Even with the dockers' mass pickets the aim has been to shut the dock gates for a limited period only. As the police, and in particular the Special Operations Division, gather, the stewards lead the women and men away from the gates in an impressive show of disciplined adherence to the chosen strategy. However, this form of picketing means that while ships are delayed (not an insignificant feature in an industry geared to meeting tight sailing and tide times), they are, nevertheless, not stopped from loading and unloading their cargoes and hence the port can still operate (though clearly with some difficulty). The picketing, therefore, has become part of a long war of attrition between the dockers and their supporters on the one hand and MDHC and the shipping and cargo lines on the other.

Mass picketing was never central to the dispute's leaders strategy and it has been further eroded as two further tactics have developed. The first was the establishment of a network of support groups throughout Britain. In many ways this developed in conjunction with the delegation work and factory and office visits that have been such an integral feature of the dispute since October 1995. This in itself did not undermine the picketing strategy and could have been the basis for developing a more sustained confrontation at the dock gates, but as it has developed the support groups have been utilised to raise money, organise delegation work and occasionally undertake pickets *away* from Liverpool (for example, at the premises of Drake International in London).[52] By December a small number of groups had been formed. The first groups were mainly created by trade union bodies and were part of the strategy to increase the active involvement of trade unionists in the dispute: to spread 'practical support'. The initiative came from activists outside the docks, trade unionists and socialists in towns and cities across the country. As the network spread, however, the emphasis has been on more 'passive' forms of support and many of the

## *Tony Russell*

*I come from a long line of dock workers. I was brought up in the west-end dock area and so the docks has always been a big part of my life. My older brother went onto the docks in 1973 but when I was 21 (old enough to go on the docks) they had stopped taking people on, so I went into the warehousing side of the industry, working for Knowsley Freight. In 1990 the company changed its name to Nelson Stevedore Company and it was taken over by MDHC - so we were brought onto the docks estate and started working ships.*

*The Nelson dockers were employed on different contracts to the main Seaforth workforce. We had different wages and conditions and would be moved around the docks to meet any shortfall in labour. Often we would be working beside MDHC's direct employees, doing the same job but getting paid less and having a poorer work regime - in this sense we were treated very much like the Torside workforce. In 1991 I was elected shop steward and saw it as an honour to represent my workmates. During the dispute I have been all over Britain and Europe raising the issues that the dispute has thrown up. I've been to Denmark, Italy and Holland and the reception we have received has always been fantastic. This fight is a fight against casualisation and for reinstatement with improved working conditions and pay for all 500 sacked dockers. MDHC have built their profits on our backs - all we are asking for is our fair share. My father fought to establish better working conditions and establish union representation. I am fighting to maintain that and to make sure that the dock industry is still there for my children if they want to work on the docks.*

groups have been located outside their original trade union base. Once again, the dominant ideas within the dispute have shaped the network's activities. The support group network remains a crucially important theme in the dockers' activity and the groups play a vital role in raising money and awareness throughout Britain. To date, three conferences have been held where the conduct of the dispute, as well as wider issues of political education have been aired (see chapter 5).[53]

The second, and by far the most important tactic to develop, has been the international strategy, developing contacts and trying to obtain international solidarity from dock communities throughout the globe. Shop stewards Jimmy Nolan and Terry Teague were central to promoting this activity which developed both as a result of the stagnation of the early weeks of the dispute and because of the belief that it is not possible to break industrial relations law. The original aims were modest, to raise money, to get statements of support and possibly some trade union action, like boycotts or go-slows, on ships and shipping lines using the Liverpool Port. However, some notable early successes [in Australia, Sweden, the US and Portugal, for example] encouraged the dockers to move further afield and contact more ports. By December 1995, flying pickets, sent to America, had obtained a statement from the American Container Line (ACL) that they would pull out of Liverpool unless a settlement was reached.[54] This victory gave further impetus to this strategy so that by January and February 1996 it had become the dominant theme of the dockers campaign (see chapter 6).

The combination of picketing, national solidarity and international boycott has increased the pressure on MDHC. Profits for the second half of 1995 were down 5 per cent[55] and by August 1996 had declined by 17.1%,[56] although this did not stop MDHC boss Trevor Furlong taking a £87,000 pay increase.[57] MDHC shares were selling for £4.84 just before the lock-out started; in August 1996 they plummeted to £3.47 and, generally throughout the last year, they have fluctuated around the £4.10-£4.30 region. The decline in profits had a direct impact on the share price and in September the shares traded around the £3.60-£3.65 mark.

Container and cargo throughput is difficult to estimate, especially as MDHC have erected a 20 foot 'iron curtain' to stop people viewing their depleted container holdings,[58] but the workforce claim through-put is substantially down on the pre-dispute era. As Bobby Morton said:

> The ships...[using the port]...are carrying 50% less cargoes...there is very little in the way of containers entering or leaving the port.[59]

## *Kevin Bilsborrow*

*I have a long family connection with the docks: my father, my grandfather and my uncles all worked there. I started when I was 21 in 1973. The working conditions on the dock began to decline rapidly after 1989, culminating in the contracts issued in 1994. The employers told us: "if you don't sign them you will be sacked". Our jobs were even advertised in the <u>Echo</u>. The contracts meant you were given a rota for a year in advance but you might as well have ripped them up for all the use they were. People received phone calls from the company both day and night changing shift times at a few hours' notice.*

*MDHC claim we are old fashioned and inflexible, yet all of the men are multi-skilled. I can drive every machine on the dock. I don't know what they mean about being inflexible, well I do, they mean they want us to work for less wages. Their idea of productivity is to grind you down into the dust, destroy your working conditions and discipline you every time you make a false move. A week before we were sacked it was plastered all over the pages of <u>Lloyds List</u> that we were the best and most efficient workforce in Europe. Yet there we were a week later sacked. Many of the men have worked on the docks for over 30 years, after all those years they deserved more than the sack. The reality is that we were the last bastions of trade unionism in the industry and they made a decision to get rid of us.*

*When you go abroad and approach dockers it doesn't take long to establish a rapport as they have the same problems, in this sense we weren't surprised that we got support but we were surprised at the level of it. When the agreement with ACL was reached in New York I was in the longshoremens' boardroom having a drink with a few dockers as they were breaking up for Christmas. The ship owners and the owners of the Stevedore companies came in for a drink and we were talking to them. They said to us 'we understand your problems, it wouldn't happen here we like to see everyone getting a piece of the pie. Everything runs smooth then.' Through a powerful union the longshoremen have good relationships with the ship owners.*

*The TGWU are hampered by Trade Union Laws. Unions are run like bureaucracies and they can lose touch with their members. Like every other unionised person in Britain I feel that the official unions should help more, and step out into the open and say these laws are bad and we are challenging them. The women and the wives have backed the men up to the hilt and we couldn't have done it without them. When your wife is backing you it feels like you are fighting for your whole family. The family know that when you are on strike you don't want to give in and the worst thing would be if you were starved back to work, so they look after you and keep your spirits up. It is a case of gritting your teeth and following through what you believe in.*

These pressures were clearly behind MDHC's second 'Final Offer' made on 25 January 1996. The basis of the second offer was a £25,000 payment to 319 men, with the rest receiving just £1,000. There were also 40 'unspecified jobs' offered. A representative of Torside Ltd was at the meeting at which this offer was made (although TGWU officials had previously been informed by MDHC that Torside had ceased trading), and offered 30 jobs to the 80 sacked Torside workforce. MDHC demanded that the offer be put to the sacked workforce via a secret postal ballot. The TGWU, despite their refusal to make the dispute official and offer the dockers and their families anything but minimal support, agreed to hold a secret ballot and suggested it was the best offer that could be obtained.[60] On the 8 February the Electoral Reform Society announced that 271 (84%) sacked MDHC workers had rejected the offer. In the week that followed similar results were obtained from the workers at Nelson Freight and Torside. The results confirmed that, as far as the dockers were concerned, this dispute is about jobs and the right to work and not money.[61]

The result of the ballot was a further boost to the confidence of the dockers, WOW and their supporters: after four and a half months the dock workforce remained solidly committed to the reinstatement campaign. The announcement was made a week before a Dockers' International Conference was held in Liverpool, comprising delegates from ports across the globe. The conference discussed the increasingly common problems of casualisation and deteriorating working conditions facing dock workers internationally, the importance of the Liverpool dispute for attempts to reverse this trend and the practical support port and dock communities throughout the world could offer the Liverpool workers (see chapter 6). The conference emphasised the 'international turn' that had been taken by the dockers and the phenomenal level of international support they had obtained. In the weeks following the conference the international strategy was pursued with even greater vigour. The aim was to increase the pressure on MDHC by obstructing vessels using the Liverpool port. In particular action was stepped up against ACL vessels in an attempt to force them to adhere to their threat to withdraw from Liverpool.

An increasingly important figure in the ACL Campaign was John Bowers, president of the (US) International Longshoremen's Association. Bowers told dockers, at their mass meeting on 13 March 1996, ACL would pull out of Liverpool when he asked them because they did not want any further disruption to their operations in the US. This was a claim that he repeated to stewards over the next few months and was relayed to dockers at their mass meetings [see, for example, Mass Meetings 29 March 1996; 19 April 1996]. There were, however, three things which delayed the ACL withdrawal. First, Bowers repeatedly warned the stewards that ACL was their best 'bargaining tool' and that they should use the threat of withdrawal to obtain talks and re-instatement. This was advice that stewards took and negotiations were entered into during April. The talks were short-lived, however, as MDHC refused to discuss any substantially new offer. At this stage the stewards asked Bowers to pull ACL out of Liverpool.

The second delaying factor was a result of MDHC's tactics and machinations. As the stewards were contacting Bowers, MDHC contacted ACL to inform them that as far as they were concerned talks were proceeding. They also organised the self-styled 'Voices of Reason',[62] a mixture of local business representatives, right-wing university professors and some community leaders, to contact Bowers and tell him what, in their opinion, ACL withdrawal would do to the economy of Liverpool. This caused confusion in America but was eventually cleared up when stewards demanded, and eventually got, a fax from the TGWU confirming that, as far as they were concerned the talks were over.

Finally, when all these issues were clarified, the Liverpool dockers expected ACL to stop using the port. However, at this point Bowers expressed concern that if ACL moved out of Liverpool their cargo may be picked up by a Canadian firm and hence American jobs on the ships and at the docks would be lost to Canada [Mass Meeting 26 April 1996]. The ACL Campaign was such a central part of the dockers' strategy in the first half of 1996 that this final delay was a substantial blow to moral. The stewards responded by immediately sending delegates to Montreal and Quebec to obtain both support and undertakings from dockers that they would not work extra ships or new vessels using Liverpool. The international campaign continued apace.

The international campaign was at the centre of the dockers' strategy and the dominance of this tactic inhibited the campaign in other areas. Indeed, if workers in Australia, America and Europe were going to blockade the Liverpool port and force MDHC into retreat, then there would seem little point in developing a local strategy. From late February and early March a recurring problem, discussed at mass meetings, has been the declining numbers involved in picketing. Thus, it would seem that the international strategy has had a direct impact on the dock gates. Other tactics have been used to publicise the dispute and maintain the pressure

## Terry Barrett

*I started on the docks in 1960 working in the office 'counting off'. When I started there were almost 21,000 people working on the docks but gradually that number has been whittled away. Severance was a great thing, it's right that if people want to leave the industry they should be looked after, but the severance should have been controlled by us - everytime someone left that job should have gone to a youngster and we could have trained them up in the job and the history of dock work. I've never been a steward but I've always been an activist. This dispute has been a long time coming - we should never have let Torside start on the docks without proper pay and conditions. It was obvious they would gradually expand their operations and force conditions down elsewhere. I've been as active as possible in this dispute. I've been up and down the country talking to workers and this is very important - workers' solidarity that is how we will win.*

## Andy Dwyer

*I started on the docks in 1962 when I was fifteen. Although my dad wasn't a docker in his job as a truck driver he delivered to the docks four times a day so he knew people who could get me a start. I have always been a union activist and have been a steward on many occasions. At the start of this dispute I was the Branch Secretary of the 610 branch of the TGWU. I have been sickened by the role of the local officials on the docks since the abolition of the NDLS and particularly since the introduction of the 1993 contracts. Although the men were given shift patterns at the beginning of each week they may have just torn them up because they never made any resemblance to the hours that they actually worked. The hours were horrendous. On many occasions we asked the union to instigate a ballot for strike action because of the way the company treated us and ignored the deal that had been made with the union. But our official generally managed to avoid having them. He was more interested in keeping in with the company than representing the men.*

*I have been really proud of the men through this whole dispute. They are highly principled people who are willing to fight for what they believe in and stick together against the employer. I have nothing but admiration for the way they stand on the picket line day after day, and it isn't just the men it is their wives and families too. The dignity has kept me optimistic and hopeful throughout the dispute. MDHC orchestrated this dipute and they don't want us back but we can't let that happen they can't win.*

on MDHC. In the run up to May Day a number of dockers proposed calling a Merseyside Day of Action but the dock stewards were reticent about issuing such a call. Eventually the demand for a day of action was taken up by trade unionists outside the docks: UNISON members throughout Merseyside voted and agreed on a 24 hour stoppage; fire-fighters, who were in dispute with the local Labour Council, intended to strike that day and local civil servants voted for strike action. There was clearly the potential for a significant show of solidarity. However, in the run up to May Day there was some confusion amongst dockers over what they were hoping to achieve. Some dockers and stewards believed they could not demand solidarity strike action (despite the building momentum) because it would mean workers breaking the law and this is something other workers would not do. As a result the wording of dockers' leaflets was softened to ask workers across Merseyside to join the early morning picket and the lunch-time demonstration and rally. There were two further blows inflicted on the Day of Action in the last few days of April. First, the fire-fighters settled their dispute and called off their strike for 1 May and second, Rodney Bickerstaff, General Secretary of UNISON, sent individual letters to his members informing them that if they took strike action and were disciplined the union would not support them. Trade union 'new realism', a mixture of ideas which emphasises that unions should work within the confines of Industrial Relations law, avoid industrial confrontation whenever possible and hope for a more union-friendly world under a Labour Government (and therefore not do anything which might be perceived to hinder Labour in a future election), clearly affected the preparation for May Day. It was behind Bickerstaff's threat to his members but it was also present in the dock stewards' approach to the day: they assumed workers would not strike in support of the dockers and, if they did, that it threatened their (albeit strained) relationship with the TGWU and with other union leaders. The success of May Day was the result of activists across the country taking action and building the campaign and this occurred in the face of prevarication by some stewards. Nevertheless, despite these problems, the May Day march and rally was one of the best supported throughout the campaign and witnessed a number of workplaces taking solidarity strike action (see chapter 5).

The combined pressures of national and international support brought a third 'Final Offer' from MDHC. This time MDHC offered a two week cooling off period when those workers wanting to take severance could leave the industry and the rest could be considered for 60 jobs in the cargo handling area with the possibility of 40 other ancillary jobs being available to former dockers. The 100 workers who would be re-employed (not re-instated) would only be employed providing they were deemed 'medically fit' and 'suitable' for the company. Clearly this was a threat against union activists and stewards. Further the 'deal' did not apply to Torside workers, though again a Torside representative suggested "some jobs" may be available. Finally, the offer was not for re-instatement but re-employment. In other words, after the initial 'cooling off' period, former dockers could find themselves re-employed as cleaners, general labourers, gig-boatmen or in any job MDHC wanted to fill. Thus, there was no guarantee of doing dock work or of earning wages and working in conditions similar to those (awful conditions) present prior to the lock-out. The new offer was rejected by the stewards after consultation with the dockers at their weekly meeting [Mass Meeting 7 June 1996].

As this offer was rejected and talks finally broke down ACL announced they would pull out of the port. Between 21 June and 24 July 1996 ACL refused to use Liverpool and, clearly, the absence of a major shipping line using the port increased the pressure on MDHC. By the same token the return of ACL on 24 July was clearly a set back for the dockers and their supporters. But as the stewards told the mass meeting on the 26 July 1996 "we have nowhere else to go".

In the face of this setback the stewards redoubled their efforts on the international front. They organised a second international conference to establish an organisational framework to aid their international activities. The aim was to locate those trade union leaders and activists within the various national trade union machineries who were concerned at the spread of casualism in the docks industry and who saw the Liverpool dispute as a crucial event in the fight against casual labour (see chapter 6). The dispute had become even more firmly tied to the international strategy for victory.

The first anniversary of the dispute was marked by activity in Liverpool and abroad. In Liverpool a large demonstration was held on Saturday 28 September followed by a mass picket at the Seaforth gates on the 30 September. The day was marked by an occupation of a section of the docks by a group of stewards and their supporters. In response, the police and OSD snatch squads arrested 32 pickets, more than had been arrested throughout the previous 12 months at the dock gates. Internationally, the first week in October saw a number of actions taken against ships, and shipping line, using Liverpool (see chapter 6). The struggle for re-instatement entered its second year on a burst of activity which disrupted the working of the Liverpool port.

In this chapter we have sketched the dockers continuing campaign. It is a campaign that has developed through three phases from a community/ public opinion campaign, to a 'traditional' union focus on picketing and attempting to obtain solidarity from other workers in the locality and, finally, to an internationally based strategy relying on the strength of dockers across the globe to close the Liverpool port. This development, however, cannot be simply compartmentalised into discrete phases - each remains in place but, after twelve months, the emphasis is clearly on the international strategy.

The resilience of the dockers and their families to fight on partially reflects the breadth and strength of the solidarity they have received. We focus on this support in chapters 5 and 6.

*The dockers march on the first rally.*
*Their banner echoes the words of the <u>Lloyds List</u> Editorial.*

*The feelings of the dockers are made clear
in this message to MDHC.*

*Dockers' picket shuts one of the port gates.*

*'Scabs' cross the picket lines.*

91

*Rejecting the February 1996 offer.*

*Faces of determination and solidarity, the Liverpool Dockers.*

# Chapter 5

*Solidarity for ever !*

As the dockers' campaign began it soon became clear that a strategy aimed at mobilising broad support from church and community dignitaries could not shame MDHC into re-instatement. Instead, there was a realisation that, if the dockers were to win, they would need to mobilise the support of other workers in Merseyside and throughout the country. As we noted in chapter 4 much of the impetus for this campaign came from trade unionists and political activists outside the docks themselves. Disputes in the docks have tended to be solid and well organised. So relying on support from other workers and developing a network of supporters and contacts did not happen automatically. Within Merseyside, many trade unionists were on hand to offer support almost immediately. As Nigel Flanagan, the local Sefton Council UNISON branch secretary told us:

> We heard about the dispute on the day they were sacked. Seaforth Dock is in Sefton Council boundaries and when we saw the picket line we went straight down and spoke to the stewards. Since then we have had regular contact with them, particularly through the Socialist Workers Party.

Steve Donnelly, AEEU convenor at AC Delco Engineering tells a similar story. Management at Delco recently threatened to close the plant down but were met by an active campaign led by the stewards which forced the company to retreat. During this dispute the dockers had offered the Delco workers substantial support so when the workforce heard about the dispute in the local media they organised a weekly levy (of at least £500) and organised to send members regularly onto the picket line. While Jane Loftus, from Liverpool CWU, said:

> word that the dockers were on strike spread throughout the local

network of political and trade union activists. Our members were keen to support the dockers in any way that they could - that meant not crossing their picket lines, starting a levy, going on their marches and on their picket lines. Symbolically, the dockers are a very important section of the working class in Liverpool and always command respect and support. This is a popular struggle and one most workers wanted to support and help the dockers win.

From further afield Martin Cock from the Kent dockers' support group heard of the dispute through the left-wing press and offered dockers accommodation and help in the Kent area - especially around the Sheerness docks which are also owned by MDHC. Such acts of solidarity were soon replicated across the country as news of the dispute spread. The dispute also won support from a range of groups and trade unionists who identified with the dockers cause and offered them various forms of support: 'practical', moral and financial. The dockers themselves viewed this support as part of a two-way process: any support they obtained would aid their victory and this in turn may encourage others to follow suit. As the dockers themselves have argued:

> We hope, that after many years of the labour movement in Britain being forced backwards, that our struggle can be an inspiration to workers in Britain and internationally to stand up and be counted.[63]

The solidarity the dockers have received can be broken down into different forms of activity. The first relates to forms of industrial or 'practical' solidarity: strikes, boycotts and go-slows which are intended to disrupt MDHC's workings and increase economic pressure on the company, thereby hastening the dockers' victory.

The immediate cause of the sacking of the majority of Liverpool dockers was their adherence to a traditional trade union principle: never cross a picket line. However, the dockers' commitment was not matched by the actions of other workers on the waterfront who continued to work normally - many being instructed to do so by their union, which in some cases, for example with lorry drivers, was the TGWU. As Irene said:

> [Bill] Morris has wagon drivers, TGWU members, going through our picket lines and TGWU members working in the docks. He is taking money from the scabs. Our men's jobs are being done by the scabs. Morris should...stop [them].[64]

Throughout the dispute the TGWU leaders' 'green light' to the scabbing operation has caused great anger amongst the dockers and their stewards [see, for example, Mass Meetings 26th April 1996, 10th May 1996]. Nevertheless, it is important to note that the potential for solidarity on the waterfront does exist. The best example is the strike days undertaken by the tugboat workers in support of their sacked colleagues.[65] The TGWU leaders, however, have been central to stifling such solidarity, arguing that the strikes are unofficial, illegal and threaten the day-to-day working of the union. Thus the real possibility of substantial secondary action on the docks, which would have effectively closed the port down and dramatically increased the pressure on MDHC, was sacrificed because the union leaders were fearful of the potential consequences of breaking the law. Such a perspective has also appeared in the statements of leading stewards [see, for example, Mass Meeting 12 April 1996]. Many of the dockers and their supporters, however, have argued that this was the time to challenge the industrial relations acts. As Paul Holleran, NUJ Scottish organiser said:

> We have the 'moral high ground' in this dispute and should not be afraid to say it..[we should choose the ground] when deciding to break industrial relations law...it must be tactically sound...this is a good case.

Des Loughney Secretary of Edinburgh Trades Council has a similar message.

> Whether you break the law or side-step the law is a tactical question in every industrial dispute. What you do depends on the circumstances...[in this case] massive support should have been organised nationally from the beginning of the dispute.

Zoe Pritchard, Kent County UNISON Branch Secretary, told us that the union leaders needed to do much more, they "should grasp the nettle and fight back". Tommy Campbell, a TGWU delegate to Aberdeen Trades Council, argued it was necessary to "[increase] the economic and industrial pressure by [undertaking] secondary action". Steve Donnelly, AEEU Convenor at Delco Electronics said:

> The anti-union laws have been a good excuse for the officials not to get the union involved...[what is needed] is secondary action like blacking haulage firms who are crossing picket lines.

While Nigel Flanagan Branch Secretary of Sefton UNISON told us:

> [anti-union laws] have provided trade union leaders with an excuse for not doing everything for the dockers...[but it is possible to break

the law] our own UNISON branch has done so many times, despite High Court injunctions. The key to winning is the support and confidence of members. The Trade Union leaders often behave [in a way that] undermines that support and confidence.

As Jane Loftus from Liverpool CWU argued:

There has been real opportunities during the dockers' dispute to involve large numbers of workers across Merseyside in a range of secondary action and of linking the dock dispute with action that has occurred in the fire service, the post office and among local government workers - the dock dispute is about basic trade union principles, things like not crossing picket lines, about the right to trade union representation and about the right to work in decent conditions. If the union leaders had stood up and made the issues clear and emphasised what the principles involved were we could have had substantial action that would have closed the port.

Many of the dockers' most active supporters from throughout the trade union movement are quite clear, then, that secondary action should have been sanctioned by the trade union leadership and that this would have speeded up the successful resolution of the dispute.

In this context we can start to comprehend the rationale behind the demand, raised by some dockers and their supporters within the dispute [see, for example, Mass Meeting 12 April 1996], for the TUC and the union leaders to make the dispute official and promote and sanction secondary action. This demand has been misunderstood as being critical of the capacities of rank and file dockers to conduct the dispute and of leading to a strategy that would force them to become subservient to the union leaders' agendas. However, this is to misread what is being sought. Although the dockers and their stewards have effectively run their dispute, years of defeat at the hands of employers and government have undermined the confidence of many workers to initiate secondary action, though such retreats have not dissipated their bitterness or anger at the employers' offensive nor undermined their willingness to take strike action when given an appropriate lead. The demand to make the dispute official and call for secondary action is intended to force the union leaders to create the conditions which will allow rank and file trade unionists to produce secondary action which will in turn increase the possibility of victory. Thus the demand is based on the claims that the trade union leaders are elected to represent their members; that the union belongs to the members and not the full time officials; that industrial relations law can and should be challenged and that union leaders have a responsibility to actively fight to save jobs and working conditions today rather than sacrificing their members' interests in the hope of courting favour with a future Labour government.

For the stewards, however, the question of the dispute being official has been less important. There is a feeling that the union has had its hands tied by legislation but that there have been times (especially when the union conducted the first ballot in February 1996 and around their continuing dominance of negotiations) when some of the stewards have questioned the TGWU's failure to make the dispute official. However, in many of the key areas of negotiation the dispute has been run as if it was official and the national officials have taken the lead role in the dealings with MDHC. Further, the stewards have turned the unofficial nature of the dispute into a virtue. They have argued that if it had been official they would not have had the freedom to run their international campaign, the central tactic of the dispute (see chapter 6).

This notwithstanding, it is the case that the practical solidarity that has been obtained has been produced by stewards, union representatives and branch officials from outside the docks. A key example surrounds the Day of Action on 1 May 1996 (see chapter 4)[66]. Although the dockers became less clear about the extent of the support they were hoping to obtain as the day of action approached (partly as a response to official union pressure and partly as a consequence of their own inaction), the day was marked by significant numbers of workers attending the morning picket, taking strike action and supporting their lunchtime march and rally. Once again the officials tried everything within their power to distance themselves from any secondary action. Sefton UNISON members voted to take strike action and attend the mass picket and rally. As Nigel Flanagan told the May Day Rally they were informed by Rodney Bickerstaff they would receive no support for such action from the official union. He went on:

> Over the last few days I have received two letters. The first letter was from Rodney Bickerstaff the General Secretary of UNISON **repudiating, repudiating** our members for daring even to discuss taking strike action in support of the dockers and threatening us with no protection whatsoever if we were taken back to the High Court!. That letter was torn up at the dockers conference on Saturday.

97

What I have now is a letter from Randan Parkins solicitors acting on behalf of the Mersey Docks and Harbour Company, threatening Sefton UNISON with legal action if we simply induce our members to turn up on the picket line this morning and turn out at the march today. Well I've got a message for the dock company not only did we induce them they turned up, they are here today, and they were here this morning!.

At this point Nigel tore up the letter.

So the key issue confronting trade unionists offering 'practical' support for the dockers has been the question of 'legality'. Many trade unionists have broken the law during the dispute and have shown a willingness to confront this issue. Further, they have not been arrested or charged for their activities, primarily because these have not been individual acts of law breaking but mass actions involving large numbers of trade unionists. However, the leadership of the trade union movement has refused to sanction such secondary actions and has done everything within its power to dissociate itself from such activities. Without such a sanctioned framework, however, the level of practical support has been limited: the reason has not been antipathy towards the dockers' cause but the heavy hand of trade union officialdom distancing themselves from traditional forms of trade union solidarity.

Further, because of the pressure from the union leadership and the nature of the restrictive anti-trade union laws the dock stewards themselves have not sought solidarity consistently from other workers. Other British ports have not been targeted for any form of solidarity action, mainly because the devastating effects of the 1989 dispute have left these ports firmly in the grip of managements who recruit only non-unionised casual labour. This has created some disagreement within the dispute, as some dockers clearly favour a more aggressive position, which calls for solidarity action from other workers, and which challenges the anti-union laws which could create the conditions for a unionisation drive in other ports. One of the ironies of the present dispute is that Liverpool dockers have gone, often unannounced, to picket workers in countries across the globe (and that includes non-unionised workers in Los Angeles, for example) yet they have not had the same confidence to undertake dock gate meetings and pickets for workers in Bristol, Tilbury or Southampton.

As we have already noted, the dominant, and collectively expressed, view within the strike committee is that solidarity action in general in Britain, and particularly in the ports, is impossible to achieve. This view has been reinforced by the TGWU leadership and from the TGWU's National Ports and Waterways Section; there has been significant pressure brought to bear on the dockers to reinforce the official position which argues that direct confrontation with existing Industrial Relations Law is impossible. In a sense, therefore, although leading a militant campaign for re-instatement and utilising a range of 'traditional' trade union methods of struggle, the strike committee reflects some *elements* of trade union 'new realism' and share the view, not held by all of their trade union supporters, that the law has effectively shackled trade unionists in Britain from providing secondary action. The acceptance of this idea has had an important effect on the way the strike committee has run the dispute, on what they have thought it possible to achieve and on the demands they have made on other workers.

As well as practical support the dockers have also looked to other trade unionists to provide financial and moral support. Running such a visible and international dispute has taken considerable financial resources - all of which have been raised by trade unionists and political activists. Internationally a number of unions have sent considerable sums to Liverpool (see chapter 6) but the main source of continuous support has been from trade unionists from throughout Britain. Some has come from regular levies given by workers, like those at Delco Engineering, Sefton UNISON or British Aerospace. Some has come as a direct consequence of activists demanding financial support at the various union conferences held throughout the year [see, for example, Mass Meeting 26 April 1996], while large amounts have been received from union branches from all over the country. This support, the majority coming as a result of initiatives from shop stewards, union representatives, convenors, branch secretaries and ordinary union members, has been essential to keep the dispute going and maintaining the dockers' spirit.

The final form of support has been 'moral' support, that is messages of support sent to the strike committee and resolutions passed supporting re-instatement at union branches, trades councils, union executives, national executive or council meetings and from union conferences. Again the level of support shown to the dockers has been quite astonishing, emphasising the level of grassroots support the dockers have.

A second strategy for solidarity has been to mobilise support outside the union machinery. They have been very successful in gaining both financial and moral support from throughout the British working class movement via its various institutions and in its various community settings.

## *Jimmy Davies Jnr*

*My grandfather was a docker and my father has been on the docks for 36 years. He has always been active in the union and is prominent in this dispute. I started on the docks in 1990 getting a job with Torside. We were taken on with the promise that our wages and general working conditions would be brought up to the level of the other dockers. However, this never happened and this was the cause of an on-going struggle with the company. In May 1995 they announced that 20 jobs had to be lost, after three months of negotiations they withdrew the redundancies but two weeks later they manufactured this dispute and sacked the entire Torside workforce.*

*I became a steward at the start of the dispute and, hence, a member of the strike committee. There is a great deal to do and I have been very busy. Each of the stewards has taken responsibility for particular tasks, even the TGWU have commented on how well the dispute has been organised. People who were really quiet before are now travelling up and down the country speaking at meetings. The Women of the Waterfront have had a great impact on the dispute, they have been involved in everything from bucket collections to picketing and are now responsible for one of the gates on their own.*

*The level of support that we have received both nationally and internationally has been magnificent. I have been to Sweden and the dockers there were saying that deregulation and casualisation was an economic wind that will blow across in their direction unless we stop it - that is why we have obtained so much international support. In Britain, when talking to other workers, they have said that they hope our struggle will provide the inspiration for others to fight back after years of deteriorating conditions. That is why this is such an important dispute.*

This has been done in two ways. First, by going into the community to raise money and support and to provide information to potential supporters about the nature and causes of the dispute. The main focus of this work has been within Liverpool itself. This has involved street collections, solidarity work with other unions and the city council, and working with other groups such as local unemployed centres and political parties. These activities have often provided the only channel through which other workers and the wider community have heard about the dispute. As Kevin commented:

> During the first weeks of the dispute we thought we were Martians because people in outlying areas of Liverpool didn't know there was a dispute in the port.

To counter this the dockers produced an A4 leaflet titled The Truth which set out the basic facts of the dispute. This was distributed widely throughout the country and was eventually translated into several different languages for delegates to take with them as they went abroad looking for support (Photostat 5). The need to publicise the dispute and its consequences also led the dockers to launch their own newspaper, The Dockers Charter, which provided information about their activities, campaign and the spread of their support group network.

Linked to this tactic the dockers have sent delegations further afield. As Terry states:

> It's my right as a trade unionist to go and ask other workers for support...and it's their duty to provide it

Initially they had difficulty gaining access to other workplaces. As a result and in order to inform workers of what was happening, they held factory gate meetings, and also held meetings with local trade councils, other union branches, as well as holding public meetings in working class communities. These activities led to the establishment of a widespread network of support groups from Aberdeen, Glasgow and Edinburgh in the north, to London, Kent and Bristol in the south. The support group held three national conferences during the first year of the dispute where the tactics being followed were discussed and future direction of support group activity outlined. This nation-wide support has been a further factor enabling the dockers to sustain the dispute.

The support network was to become increasingly important throughout 1996. They provided accommodation for dockers and WOW members when they travelled to meetings; they raised money to sustain the dispute;

## MERSEYSIDE DOCKWORKERS' DISPUTE

# THE TRUTH

500 Liverpool dockers have been sacked by their employer, the Mersey Docks & Harbour Company, after they engineered the dismissal of 80 young dockers so that they could replace them with casual workers.

Liverpool dockers, many of them with over 40 years service, have been issued with their P45s. This is a disgrace!

Industrial relations have been a problem in the Port since 1989. We have had mass disciplines, final warnings, de-recognition of shop stewards, falling safety standards, threats of dismissal, and more.

The Mersey Docks & Harbour Company is a bad employer who refuses consistently to discuss problems, in preference to using threats and intimidation. They have abused their power in a most disgraceful manner.

Liverpool docks is one of the most profitable and successful ports in the U.K., with profits in excess of £35 million, handling more cargo than in its heyday of the 1950s, with a turnover of £130 million. For a lifetime, dockers have worked in this Port as did their fathers and now their sons (who were the first to be sacked. We load and discharge ships. We make the profits.

Since 1989 tax payers' money has been used to featherbed the directors of the Company. £112 million in 1989 Over £200 million of tax payer's money was used to make dockers redundant in 1989 across the UK. Millions of pounds of tax payer's money has been poured into the dock company vaults in the form of Objective I Status (Euro grants as well as City Challenge money). We welcome all investment in the Port in the hope that it creates secure and real employment for the people of Merseyside. In effect, the MDHC from the tax payers investment is a nationalised port and it belongs to the people of Merseyside. It is no surprise to dockers to hear that the "Finance Director of the MDHC" resigned on Wednesday.

(Photostat 5)
*The Truth*

## *Bob Richie*

*I have worked on the docks for five years, for the Torside company. From the very beginning the attitude of the management at Torside was appalling. For example. although our basic working week was 40 hours, the men often worked 70 to 80 hours. This overtime was not voluntary, if you refused to do it you were threatened with discipline or the sack.*

*I have spent a lot of time travelling round Britain during this dispute particularly in Scotland. My wife has also been heavily involved in all parts of the campaign including delegation work. The importance of the work and support provided by the women can not be overstated. I have addressed over 700 meetings, including trade councils, support group meetings, public meetings, union meetings and the Scottish TUC Conference. The delegation work has been very important in allowing us to inform people what is going on in Liverpool as the press cover has been virtually non-existent: it was especially bad at the beginning of the dispute.*

*The eyes of people are on Liverpool. There is not one group of workers that I have spoken to who did not feel that their working conditions had been under attack over the last 10 years. They are willing us to win and this is reflected in the amount of moral and financial support we have received and continue to receive from up and down the country. This support has been tremendous.*

members took resolutions of support into their own unions, and they organised campaigns in their own area against the dockers main protagonists: MDHC, the American Container Line (ACL) and Drake International. Such campaigns took various forms. In London the headquarters of Drake's were occupied and the Stock Exchange was picketed and leafleted about MDHC and the dispute; in Kent a campaign was waged around the Sheerness Docks; while just outside Glasgow, the Greenock Port, which was taking some Liverpool traffic, was being used to undermine the Portugese dockers' support campaign (see chapter 6), banners supporting Liverpool dockers were unfurled from the gantries.

The contacts the dockers have established across the country have provided the means to financially sustain and run the dispute (at a cost of approximately £30,000 per week). It has established a network of activists keen to provide whatever support they can to aid the dockers' cause. It has been central to building the dockers' demonstrations and ensuring that the demonstrations have representatives and banners from across the country. Finally, the breadth of popular support obtained by the dockers has made it difficult for the official trade union movement to wash their

hands of their struggle. The trade union leaders have not actively built support for the dockers or sanctioned secondary action but the activities of the dockers and their supporters have made it impossible for the official movement to sweep them under the carpet. It has also created the framework of support to sustain the dispute and allowed the dockers to develop and maintain their international strategy. It is the international strategy that we focus on in chapter 6.

*(Top)*
*One year into the dispute,*
*workers and supporters come*
*to Liverpool in their thousands*
*to demonstrate their solidarity*
*with the Liverpool Dockers*
*and their families 28th*
*September 1996.*

105

*Tony Benn , one of the few members of 'New Labour' to support the dockers, addresses the December 1995 rally.*

*Solidarity on the Waterfront*

*Workers and supporters gather to listen to the speech
of Tony Benn at the December 1995 Rally.*

*Workers from across Britain come to Liverpool to support the
Liverpool Dockers and their families, 23ʳᵈ March 1996.*

*Arthur Scargill addresses the Liverpool rally
on 23rd March 1996.*

(Above)
Workers from Merseyside
and all around Britain
gather on May Day 1996
to show their support for
the Liverpool Dockers.
Sefton Unison members
defied instructions from
Rodney Bickerstaff not to
attend this rally.

(Right)
Paul Foot addresses the May Day
Rally quoting Shelley to great
applause: "Rise like lions after
slumber in unvanquishable number,
shake your chains to earth like dew
which in sleep has fallen on you. We
are many they are few!"

109

*Banners from across Britain show the depth of support from workers for the Liverpool Dockers and their families, 28th September 1996.*

# Chapter 6

## *Global Warfare*

One of the distinctive features of the present dispute has been the dockers' international strategy.[67] The dockers and shop stewards have developed contacts with shop stewards, union port officials and trade union leaders in a number of ports and countries throughout the globe. The dockers receive differing forms of support from workers in ports stretching from Australia and New Zealand in the south to Sweden and Norway in the north; from Japan, parts of Russia, West and Central Europe and from Canada and America. Delegates have been sent to picket docks in, amongst other places, Vancouver, New York, Le Havre, Piraeus, Auckland and Melbourne. Solidarity has also been obtained from workers in Portugal, Tenerife, Spain, Ireland and Sweden. Perhaps the key reason for this success is that the issue of casualisation on the ports is an increasingly international problem and overseas dock workers can easily and immediately identify with the problems faced by the Liverpool workers and their families.

The port workers have looked to the international dock labour force for support, in order to create the means to prevent cargo bound for Liverpool being dealt with, therefore causing maximum disruption to MDHC. This has resulted in tremendous moral, financial and practical international support, and produced solidarity action including go-slows and boycotts of ships bound for or coming from Liverpool. This international strategy is an innovative tactic and has borne some notable successes; in particular it has established a network of dock activists prepared to undertake physical support of workers in different countries, and by producing such solidarity it has increased the pressure on companies using the Liverpool docks and impacted upon MDHC's ability to run the Liverpool port.

The success of the international campaign can be seen in the reactions of some of the most prominent shipping lines in the Liverpool port who

## *Bobby Morton*

*My father was a registered docker and a shop steward with the TGWU,when he first began working on the dock the men were selected out of pens. I started on the docks in 1966 when I was 16. I went in straight from school and it is the only job that I have ever had. I worked on the clerical side although after the abolition of the NDLS in 1989 everyone was classed as a port worker . I first became a steward in the early 1980's.*

*When the P45 notice dropped through the door I remember the four of us, my wife, two children and myself, being together and crying, it was at that moment the reality hit home. That happened on the Friday, on the Monday my wife and I got the kids ready for school and as soon as they went out of the door my wife got very upset. I have a 15 year old son who has a can of coke waiting for him in the fridge when he gets home from school. On that morning he had told his mother: 'I know things have got to change, so from now on I'll have a glass of water instead of a can of coke.' It sounds a silly thing but it was a marvellous expression of his support. I have been incredibly lucky with my family. As soon as the dispute started I got them together and explained what had happened, why it happened and what I needed to do. I have had in excess of 100% support from day one and that has never waned.*

*About eight weeks into the dispute we decided upon the international strategy. The international support wasn't handed to us on a plate we had to work for it. My first trip to the east coast of America with Kevin and Tony was like an emotional roller coaster. We followed the Atlantic Conveyor across the ocean. We were told if we set up a picket line in Baltimore it would be honoured. But we landed in the middle of an inter-union dispute and the picket was only partially successful: the clerical staff didn't cross the line, those who were working the ship did. It was terribly disappointing . We followed the ship to Norfolk, Virginia. This was a dreadful experience. The police told us to get out of the place as quickly as possible. Initially we persisted and said we were staying but they told us that if we didn't get out immediately we would be thrown into their prison, which would be unlike anything we had experienced. They added, that no one would be able to come along and get us out within a day or two and that we would disappear in their system until they wanted to let us out. We were ready to return home at this point and felt very low. However Kevin's passport was stolen and while we were waiting for this to be sorted out it was suggested to us that we should picket Newark, New Jersey where the ship had just docked. As we set up the picket line, at 6am on a December morning in the fiercest blizzard for 70 years, we didn't know what to expect. When the first longshoreman came to the gate, we approached his car and explained our situation. He turned back and that happened with every longshoreman we approached. The feeling that we had when this happened was one of elation: we were dancing on the picket line, we were intoxicated, even though we hadn't been drinking. We maintained that picket line for the best part of a week and subsequently ACL put pressure on MDHC which forced them into negotiations.*

have put pressure on MDHC to end the dispute. The American company ACL (American Container Line), the largest company using the port, repeatedly threatened to leave the port because of the threat made by American longshoremen that they would refuse to work ships bound for Liverpool. This pressure was clearly behind MDHC's move, after four months of the dispute, to meet Bill Morris and the TGWU and make an offer to reinstate 40 men and provide redundancy payments of up to £25,000 to the Seaforth dockers (see chapter 3). Continuing international pressure was also behind the second 'final offer' of limited re-employment made in May 1996. However, the continuing prevarication of MDHC, the threat of international disruption to ACL and the reality of delayed ships in Liverpool and Sweden, eventually led ACL to leave the port of Liverpool on 21 June 1996.

The creation of an international strategy was seen by the shop stewards committee as essential for the success of the dispute. As the months have progressed it has taken the centre stage in their pursuit of victory and has been the major focus of the dockers' energies and activities. As Jimmy Nolan said to us:

> As you know over the past nine months our struggle has been predominantly based on internationalism.

The decision to create this strategy was taken after the dispute had been running for five or six weeks. Two reasons are put forward by the stewards when asked why this decision was made. First, Terry Teague, the steward primarily responsible for the organisation of the international campaign points out, that the decision:

> To move onto the international scene was taken in some respects out of sheer frustration against unfair and one sided labour laws that operate throughout the UK. With no secondary or solidarity action forthcoming from our normal allies, such as other waterways workers both nationally or locally, as well as the other big industrial workers like Fords, Vauxhall and other transport workers.[68]

The strike committee believed that it would be impossible to achieve significant physical support within Britain. They saw the primary reason for this as the anti-trade union legislation currently in place in Britain which they believe has undermined the ability of workers to support their campaign through solidarity action. This view does not necessarily reflect the views of all the dockers (as we discussed in chapters 1, 2 and 4) and it perhaps also underestimates the potential for solidarity within Britain (as we noted in chapter 5).

## Tony Nelson

*I started on the docks in 1973 when I was 16. My father who retired in 1983 was a docker for 40 years. I have always worked on the clerical side of dock work. In 1988 I went to work at the Seaforth dock in the import and export section. Although those of us in the office were not part of the National Dock Labour Scheme we, to an extent, felt protected by it through association. We always supported the dockers if they were in dispute and they supported us.*

*After the abolition of the NDLS I remember clearly the first day back. Everyone was given a brush, there were 400 people brushing up. I and many others understood the symbolic nature of this gesture. Conditions of work were continually eroded for the next four years. Finally in 1994 the company were allowed to impose an agreement which was never going to work. Discipline procedures became the way in which they enforced this agreement. This dispute had been coming for a long time. From day one it was about casualisation and privatisation on the ports it was never just about Torside.*

*My abiding memory of this dispute will be the opportunity it has given me to travel around the world. I first went to Montreal for a week and on the first day the thing that hit me was not that this was similar to the Port of Liverpool but that it was exactly the same. The men are the same, the culture is the same, even though they are French Canadians: they toss up in the pen to see who is on and who is off, they go down the pub, they argue with their mates, they work the same machinery, father follows son into the industry. One port is exactly the same as another, I had never really realised that.*

*As I meet these people from different parts of the world, who I thought were so different, I realised that we are part of the same working class, with the same ideas, goals, and dreams.*

The second reason which the stewards cite for pursuing the international strategy springs from the commonality of the work experience of dockers around the world. Dock work is the same across the globe and dockers internationally are facing a similar onslaught from privatisation and casualisation. Furthermore, dockers internationally are working ships operated by the same lines around the world. In these circumstances the stewards have argued:

> With so many things in common between workers, such as the jobs we perform i.e. working down the holds of ships, the driving of plant and equipment, office working, the method of hire, the central meeting place and fair systems of work and manning scales which are similar the world over from Sydney to Salerno. If we align these points to common employers such as the big shipping companies and the strong role and belief that dock workers have with their own various trade unions, and then link those issues to the global problems of casualisation and privatisation, international solidarity between dock workers of the world, should really be our first course of action and not our last.[69]

The creation of international links between dock workers is not a wholly new phenomenon. During the 1970's and 1980's, conferences of European dockers had been held in Birmingham, Barcelona, Tenerife and Antwerp. Within Britain the delegates to these conferences were organised by the National Port Shop Stewards' Committee, which was an unofficial rank and file body with strong support from all UK ports. As well as having European-wide meetings, conferences were also organised on a zonal basis so dockers from countries such as Britain, Ireland, Spain, Italy, Germany, Holland, and Sweden could meet to discuss common trading and labour links. Thus although the present tactic is 'innovative' in so far as it has developed significant international support, it was able to develop because of previous contact and links between dockers and ports.

The international tactic has developed over the months of the dispute. Initially the aim was to inform port workers around the world about the nature of the attack that was being made upon the dockers in Liverpool and to highlight this as the latest step in the casualisation of port work world-wide by governments, dock companies and ship owners. Although this message has been conveyed to dockers through the international delegations, activists and workers across the globe have also been informed by the creation of a home page on the World Wide Web. This use of modern technologies has been an important tool in disseminating information about the strike to supporters across the globe.

Initially it was hoped that the move to an international strategy would supplement the moral and financial support that the dockers were already receiving from Britain. This has clearly been highly successful and letters, faxes, and phone calls continue to arrive on a daily basis pledging moral and financial support. The dockers have received money from port workers from such diverse countries as Norway and Japan. There are some examples of substantial financial support. For example, Japanese workers sent one million yen for the dispute fund; the International Longshoremen and Warehousemen's Union of America has contributed almost US$100,000; dockers from Genoa (Italy) have pledged to donate an hour's overtime each month to the dockers until the end of the dispute and money has been sent from Belgium, Israel, Norway, Finland, France, Denmark, New Zealand, Canada, Spain, Sweden, Ireland and many other countries. This can be seen as a substantial victory for the international campaign. It is also a source of continued hope and confidence about the dispute's outcome. As Terry says:

> the moment we started to gain international support it encouraged everyone from the shop stewards' movement right down to the ordinary rank and file. Every time we get a message of support it gives us a boost.

However, as the dispute has progressed the unfolding international strategy has altered to include a perspective of obtaining international physical support via campaigns boycotting ships and goods bound for Liverpool. To win such support the dockers have emphasised the similarities of increasing attacks on working conditions in many ports and to argue that it is imperative for dockers internationally to make a stand through solidarity action with the Liverpool dockers. Their aim is to create a total blockade on the ships originating from, and destined for, Liverpool and they have asked their fellow workers to refuse to work on any such ships, or, if this is not possible, to delay the turn around time of the vessels. The purpose of this action was to bring as much financial pressure to bear on MDHC in order to bring them to the negotiating table and reinstate the sacked men.

The key to building this support depended on sending delegations of dockers around the world so that they could explain their case and outline the nature of the solidarity action which they needed. Financing this international work is a testament to the strength of the support that the dock dispute has attracted both in Britain and abroad. At the start of the dispute the cost of trips was covered by money donated by local and national support groups, individuals and fellow trade unionists. However, once news of the dispute spread it was the unions in various countries around the world who invited the dockers to come to see them as their guests and provided expenses to cover the trips.

Initially the dockers sent people to what were considered 'friendly ports' where previous contacts had been made. The first delegation was to Bilbao in Spain where Liverpool has a container trade through Ellerman's Andrew Weir shipping lines. It was also important to make contact with ports which had a significant direct trade link with Liverpool, and so delegations were sent to ports in Canada where the shipping lines CAST ,CANMAR and BALTIC were based, to Sydney in Australia where ABC Lines operates and, most importantly of all, to the East Coast of America where the biggest shipping line using Liverpool, ACL, operates. The position of ACL was to become a central measure of the success of the international campaign.

These initial delegations brought a high degree of success. Financial and moral support was obtained at all the ports visited and boycotts started in Sweden and New Zealand. In Canada delegations were sent to Montreal, Toronto and Quebec with the result that ships loaded in Liverpool were boycotted.

In Australia delegates went to 21 meetings including 10 mass meetings of working dockers. The result was a series of go-slows and 24 hour delays on the ABC shipping line, who normally shipped between 600 and 700 containers per trip through Liverpool, and who, partly as a result of this action, were soon to cease trading. Finally the visit to the USA included three Liverpool dockers setting up a picket in Newark, New Jersey. The anti-union laws in the USA are even more draconian than those in Britain and the official longshoremen's union could play no role in raising the dispute with their members. Nevertheless, the dockers set up their picket line, talked to the longshore workers as they approached the dock gates and turned the dockers away - a quite amazing act of international solidarity and an event which conflicts with many British people's views of American workers. The Liverpool workers had previously chased an ASL vessel up and down the east coast of America to Maryland, Baltimore and Virginia. ACL took legal action against the Liverpool men who found themselves in a US court at the centre of a Fifth Amendment dispute. Yet despite these trials, the support of US workers remained solid and ACL agreed to pull out of Liverpool if negotiations failed. This was the most substantial victory achieved from the first round of international visits and gave the whole dispute a massive boost at the right time, Christmas 1995.

117

Perhaps the key factor sustaining the international campaign is that the issue of casualisation on the ports is an increasingly international problem and that the overseas dock workers can easily and immediately identify with the problems faced by the Liverpool workers and their families. As Kevin, one of the delegates to America, commented:

> What did surprise us was the level of the support we got, it was tremendous, but the similarity of the problems, the immediate understanding of how you work and what problems you are going through as a result of casualisation [and] attacks by bosses - that didn't surprise me at all.

The hard work and dedication put in by those who have travelled overseas has been vital. It has been an entirely new experience for many of the delegates, drawn from the shop stewards, rank and file dockers and women from WOW. In visiting overseas ports they have had to talk to workers who were often initially suspicious of who they were, and have often also struggled in terms of translation. These have not been holidays but important jobs of work involving talking to mass meetings, union officials and employers. As Terry states:

> It is also important to recognise the courage of the delegates that went all over the world. It's alright sitting on a plane, but it is when you get off the plane, probably in a country they have never been to, without any proper arrangements being made, and doing an important job of work like they did,...[that]... was down to the calibre of the individuals who went out there dealing with Presidents of unions and ordinary dock workers.

In some situations delegations have been sent to other countries without prior arrangements being made and on these occasions dockers left Britain uncertain of the reception they would receive when they stepped off the plane. The example of Brian and Derek is not untypical. They went to France where they were met by some (initially disgruntled) local union officials. They slowly explained the case of the Liverpool dockers over the following few hours and were eventually promised support and access to the docks. When inside the docks the language problem increased (because there was now no translator) but soon garbled French, garbled English and an impromptu sign language created bonds of friendship and solidarity between the dockers. As Derek said: "the pens are the same, the work is the same, we are the same." As he said (to general laughter) in his report back to the mass meeting (9 Feb. 1996):

all they kept saying was: "le courage, le courage, le courage" - and that means courage lads.

The international visits have exposed the delegates to new experiences, taken them to places they never thought they would go, have forged friendships amongst new comrades across the globe and have created 'international ambassadors' for the working class of Liverpool. The delegates have grown and developed in ways that they would never have dreamt possible before the dispute and are an important modern symbol of the international brother and sisterhood of labour.

On the back of their international campaign the shop stewards organised an international conference of dock workers and their immediate representatives. The purpose of the conference was to consolidate the links that had been made, to discuss the common problems facing dockers internationally and explore possible solutions, including the possibility of creating a world-wide dockers' union. The conference took place in Liverpool from the 18 to 23 February 1996. It is perhaps worth noting that the TGWU did not want to be involved in the conference and would not give permission for Transport House in Liverpool to be used as a venue. As a result the event was held in Liverpool Town Hall. As was mentioned earlier, conferences of dock workers had been held before but, as the strike committee noted:

> This conference...will be the first...International Conference, to our knowledge, that will cover port workers from all over the world with nearly all the major ports being represented.[70]

There were fifty-five delegates from 18 countries and 24 resolutions of support and solidarity between dockers were unanimously agreed promising international disruption of the ships using the Liverpool port. A number of the ITF (International Transport Federation) Inspectors were also at the conference and they passed the following resolution:

> Having heard the report given by the representatives of the sacked Liverpool dockers, we the ITF Inspectors present at this 1996 world-wide seminar condemn the sacking of the 500 Liverpool dockers by the MDHC. We call upon our respective unions throughout the world to organise industrial action including boycott actions in their respective ports and countries against any vessel known to be loading/discharging cargoes from the port of Liverpool.

The role of individual inspectors has been important in helping to delay certain ships during the course of this dispute. However apart from passing resolutions the ITF have not enacted any significant solidarity action.

# Tony Melia

*I started on the docks in May 1991, I was one of the first intake of 30 men to
Torside. I first became a steward in July 1993. For my money the dispute started
long before it kicked off. Just prior to the dispute we had a ballot over redundancies,
the firm wished to make 20 full timers redundant while retaining a part time work
force that they had recruited in 1993. We were opposed to that, the ballot showed
95% against. The firm withdrew the redundancies, we considered that a moral
victory but we weren't naive enough to think something else wasn't coming. We
weren't surprised at the way in which people were sacked from Torside, it was
typical of their macho management style.*

*The dispute is run from the shop stewards' committee and everyone has their
niche. Jimmy Davies Jr and myself have been involved in the organising the social
aspects of the campaign. We were chiefly responsible for the organisation of the
Dockers Summer Festival which raised £7,000 in one day.*

*I have also been involved in many international delegations including those to
New Zealand, Australia and Cuba. In the beginning it was quite daunting. We
normally went in pairs but when Kevin and I went to New Zealand we were split
up. I remember one occasion when I had been taken to have lunch with the general
executive of one of the unions. When we arrived at the Chinese Restaurant there
were about 12 people there and I was the youngest. The bloke I was with introduced
me as Tony from Liverpool. I thought I'll never remember all those names so, a
typical Scouser, I thought, 'keep your mouth shut until you can suss everyone out',
then the fella next to me, who was an older docker, started asking me about the
dispute. After about five minutes he said 'hang on, hang on' then he turned to
everyone else and said: 'hey lads, have you heard what he is saying, this is what is
happening here.' That broke the ice and they started asking me lots of questions.
Someone said during the dispute that dockers are the same people across the
world even if they speak a different language- from what I've seen, there is definitely
an affinity between dock workers around the world.*

*My wife and family have been very supportive. Collette's grandad was a docker
and she is on the WOW committee and her mum and sister are also in WOW. The
kids have been to every march, every vigil, every mass picket and every rally. They
are fully conversant with what is going on. I went into school the other day to see
my kids' work and my lad had written this thing about the docks. He wasn't referring
to me but to the older men how they had lost everything and how they had come
out to support 'my dad' when he got sacked. I was almost in tears. The teacher
had written 'absolutely brilliant' at the bottom. He is nine years old. Collette has
worked tremendously hard during the dispute. She has a full time job as a staff
nurse and has fitted all the work she does for WOW, including going to Sweden on
delegation work, around this.*

*The outcome has got to be total victory not just for the dockers but for the whole
working class movement.*

On the Wednesday the delegates joined the dockers in a mass international picket of the Seaforth gate. As one of the British dockers said at the Mass Meeting 23 Feb. 1996:

> The international conference took place over five days... we had a blank day on the Wednesday and I felt it was the most important day of the whole conference. When the delegates actually went down to the picket lines...that was for me, the best day of the conference. One of our Spanish colleagues said to me that 'the conference is very good but this is where it is, on the picket lines, that is where we will win it'.

And as one of the delegates from New Zealand argued: "On Wednesday we had the opportunity to see trade unionism at its best."

There was also discussion about the possibility of establishing a dockers' international union. This reflected the shared antipathy towards trade union officialdom. As the German delegate to the conference said:

> Your officials are mostly like ours, they sit behind closed doors and you don't know what they are talking about and you have to try and fight and struggle in your own way.

While the Greek representative argued:

> One thing I don't understand these people who are supposed to support the working class they sit in their offices. They have forgotten where they come from. They should be here side by side with the dockers.

The morale and the optimism amongst the dock workers was further boosted by the success of the conference. Everyone that we have spoken to saw it as one of the high points of the dispute. The depth of feelings which were demonstrated during this week are best reflected in the words of the delegates themselves as they addressed the mass meeting in Transport House on 25 February. As Terry, representing the stewards, said:

> We have been able to do something people thought we couldn't do. When we commenced this strike we recognised fully that one of the ways we were going to win this strike was to take our strike internationally. People scoffed and scorned at us and said dock workers won't be able to do that. We weren't backed by any official union we were 500 dockers on our own but we had the confidence, confidence instilled in us by your decision not to cross a picket line.

The Irish representative argued:

The situation we had in Derry is very similar to the one you had here where the employers wanted just to smash the union in our port as they want to smash it here they could be carbon copies...You have had our solidarity from day one and you will continue to have it until the final conclusion of this dispute...when you will march back to work victorious, unbowed, unbloodied and undefeated.

The Portuguese worker said:

What you are doing here is not only for you but for all dockers... From Lisbon to Liverpool until you win no more cargo.

While the Swedish activist stressed:

It was a very easy decision for us in the Swedish Dock Workers' Union to support you  not only through financial aid but through a blockade on all goods to and from Liverpool.....what happened to you in late September could happen to us in Sweden. Your fight today could be our fight tomorrow...Workers with fighting spirit and dignity are very frightening for the bosses and the ruling class.

As the Italian delegate stated: "the language of the worker, when you are doing the same job, is the same all around the world."

The Australian representative said:

[Y]ou turned this from an ordinary struggle into a world-wide political dispute.....you have turned this dispute...into what is going to be the starting stone of what we do in Australia- coming back and fighting back.

The Canadian delegate stressed that:

We are going to make sure that the message of the Liverpool dockers is also spread throughout the world to every port that we can possibly contact and tell them the story of the Liverpool dockers and their families. You have our pledge on that.

The Danish dockers pledged similar support:

On Tuesday there will be a meeting of three or four hundred shop stewards from all over Denmark. I will take this resolution and explain the Liverpool situation to gain support from across Denmark.

While from France they said:

We are in a hurry to get back to France and tell our brother dockers about your plight and they will take action for you.

The German dockers said:

We are going to do something with the ACL and CANMAR ships. We will stop them and boycott them, I promise you.

While the Greek docker stated:

We will express our solidarity whenever and however that is possible. When we return to Greece we will carry on the solidarity by applying the decisions and resolutions of this conference and we have to apply the pressure whenever and where ever it is needed and we will wait to hear the message of victory in Liverpool which is a victory for all of us.

Summing up the conference and the dispute the Australian delegate argued:

Your victory will further enrich the great working class history of Liverpool. Your victory will be a victory for every decent man and woman throughout the world the final successful conclusion of this dispute will enhance further the concept of internationalism unity and solidarity cemented here this week.

For the stewards, the conference was important for three reasons. First, it enabled the dockers to show MDHC that they had substantial international support which could be used to disrupt ships using the Liverpool port. Second, it boosted the dockers' confidence: the talk of internationalism seemed to be justified and seemed to hold out the possibility that concerted effort by Swedish, Italian, Portugese, Greek, American and Australian dockers would win the dispute for the Liverpool workers. Finally, if the dockers won, it could herald the start of a significant international rank and file movement which could be used to support workers in other ports.

After the conference the international work continued with delegations travelling around the world working hard to maintain the momentum. French railway workers invited dockers to speak to their conference where they were concerned at what they termed the spreading 'British disease': unemployment, casualisation and government attacks on benefits [Mass Meeting 22 March 1996]. In Portugal, the dockers' booklet <u>Never Cross A Picket Line</u> has been translated into Portuguese and distributed across the various docks (which are covered by 12 trade unions). Partly as a result Portuguese dockers stepped up their campaign of boycotting Liverpool bound cargoes [Mass Meeting 15 March 1996]. Thus, the solidarity, both financial and physical, promised at the conference

123

continued to build, but the strike committee would concede that this had not always been as consistent as they would have liked. Further, the practical support they have obtained has been sporadic, uneven and often short lived. The long-running campaign to remove ACL from the port and the short-term success of June/July 1996, seems to emphasis the difficulties (see chapter 4). The reasons for this include the responses of the various employers around the world and concern by dockers that cargoes that they turn away may be dealt with in other ports. The role of the ITF in co-ordinating this action, especially in Europe, has not materialised and on occasion has been openly obstructive (for example instructing the Belgian and German delegates not to attend the second international conference in Liverpool, see below). However, some individual ITF inspectors have continued to play a role in delaying shipping.

However there also continue to be success stories. An example was the trip to the West Coast of America where the delegates set a picket on Los Angeles Port, the third biggest in the world. No one crossed the line and negotiations held with the employer resulted in all the Longshoremen being paid for their shift while they were on strike!

The far reaching international effects of this dispute were never more clearly demonstrated than by the action of a group of Mexican truck drivers who had honoured picket lines set up in Los Angeles by Liverpool dockers even though they were non-unionised and were risking their livelihood. They went on to set up their own union. As Bobby told marchers at the May Day Rally:

> [A]mongst the people who refused to cross that picket line [in LA] were a large number of Mexican truck drivers who didn't belong to any union whatsoever. We are very thankful to them for not crossing but the reason I mention it is that we received a telephone call from LA last night to say that those workers who are amongst the lowest paid workers in America learnt a lesson from that picket line and set up a picket line of their own which paralysed the whole of the LA docks for 24 hours and those people are joining the union. It is just an example of why we are going and why ship owners and employers around the world are asking Mersey Docks and Harbour Company why did you open this can of worms which is now threatening to ignite the whole of the trade union movement around the world.

124

As well as the ACL campaign (see chapter 4), the dockers have also tried to increase the pressure on Canadian Pacific, who own both the CANMAR and CAST shipping lines. In late June 1996 CANMAR vessels withdrew from the port. This was a major victory for the dockers and, as a consequence, the financial position of the MDHC plummeted. The dockers then focussed attention on the CAST shipping line. CAST's direct managers made it clear that they would not leave Liverpool and so the dockers started a specific campaign aimed at forcing them out of Liverpool and, as a consequence, more or less shutting the port completely. The first shots in this campaign were fired in the week beginning 14 July 1996 when four dockers went to Canada in an attempt to disrupt CAST's operations. The anti-union restrictions in Canada make it almost impossible for workers to legally offer solidarity action with workers in struggle. In these circumstances the dockers decided to take action themselves. The four walked into the docks with the morning shift, climbed a gantry and unfurled a massive banner which read "CAST uses scab labour in Liverpool". Police and security officers were called and tried to talk the men down, but they refused until they received guarantees that they could talk to local union officials and to the local CAST managers. This was eventually obtained and the men came down to be met by Canadian dockers who formed a circle around them to protect them from the police who tried to arrest them. The men had their meeting in which they informed CAST of their intention to step up action against the company until they withdrew from the port. They also obtained promises of support from the dock unions and received a large amount of publicity in the Canadian media. The day finished with the men being arrested and deported from Canada but feeling the trip had been worthwhile and an important first engagement [Mass Meeting 19 July 1996].

The return of ACL to Liverpool did not lead the dockers to question the international strategy. Instead they felt that with a little more effort they could instigate a significant boycott of the port. Hence, they re-doubled their efforts to extend and strengthen the international campaign. As part of this process, a second international conference was organised for the weekend of 31 August 1996. The purpose of this conference was twofold: first, to strengthen the existing international ties between dock workers and provide the next step towards creating an 'international rank and file movement'; and secondly, to focus on the nature of the support that had been offered to Liverpool and explore how it could be consolidated and extended. With this in mind the aim was to attract delegates from ports

**Adopted resolution to be submitted to each country's own organisations for ratifiction.**

Conference calls upon the ITF and affiliates to work towards the 30th September for an international day of action.

To begin a co-ordinated campaign to hit all ACL/CAST traffic and container together with other shipping consortiums on a worldwide basis that use the port of Liverpool and Medway.

To organise immediately visits To Germany by Liverpool, Danish and Swedish dockers, to Belgium and Holland by Liverpool and French dockers - to seek their support for co-ordinated action.

To agree a rolling programme of action using delegates from Liverpool in Northern Europe, America and Canada and Southern Europe in successive weeks, beginning in the week of (dates for each area to be decided by conference) to seek their support for action such as boycotts, slow-downs (go-slows) and all other methods dockers are familiar with which can affect productivity and efficiency on Ellerman, Zim, Cast and Canmar

To organise visits to Cyprus, Greece, Turkey and Israel to co-ordinate action in this area against Gracechurch, Ellermans and Zim.

To organise in all ports regular weekly collections, on the lines of the Swedish dockers, if this is applicable to each port's traditions. For confrence delegates to sign a joint appeal with the sacked Liverpool dockers for worldwide circulation, calling on the ITF and affiliates to support.

VICTORY TO THE LIVERPOOL DOCKERS!
VICTORY TO DOCKERS WORLDWIDE!

**Delegates undertake to pursue these objectives in their respective ports and countries.**

Sydney:

Montreal:

Arhus

Copenhagen

Le Havre

Tarragona

Bilbao

Sweden

Portland, Oregon

St. Johns, New Brunswick

Liverpool

SALERNO

1st September 1996

(Photostat 6a)
*Conference resolutions*

**Adopted resolution to be submitted to each country's own organisations for ratifiction.**

Internationalism has a historical resonance for all dock workers.

Following our experience of two international dockworkers' conferences, the need to formalise this conference is apparent.

This alliance has to be developed and this objective has been agreed.

The democratic alliance of dock workers internationally will be achieved. The necessary constitutional structure shall be developed forthwith through an elected Steering Committee temporarily established to oversee this work.

This Steering Committee shall be composed of elected delegates as per resolution 13 carried at the February Conference 1996.

Delegates undertake to pursue these objectives in their respective ports and countries.

Sydney:

Montreal:

Arhus

Copenhagen

Le Havre

Tarragona

Bilbao

Sweden

Portland. Oregon

St. Johns. New Brunswick

Liverpool

SALERNC .

1st September 1996

(Photostat 6b)

127

which had trading links with Liverpool, or which could potentially handle re-directed work. Delegates came from 12 ports in 9 countries (Sweden, Denmark, France, Canada, Italy, Spain, USA, Australia and England.) Dockers representatives were also expected from both Belgium and Germany. Support from both countries was important as there were fears that ships turned away from Spain and France would re-route to these ports. In the weeks immediately prior to the conference delegates were sent to these countries in order to secure their presence and, in both countries, after meeting Liverpool dockers union officials promised to send representatives to the conference. The dockers were particular pleased that Bob Baete, President of the Belgian Transport Workers' Union, was now apparantly supporting their struggle. Unfortunately neither of the dock workers' unions in these two countries actually attended the conference. They are both ITF affiliates and had been contacted by the ITF and told that the conference did not have their support because the ITF believed that the Liverpool workforce was at the forefront of an attempt to create an alternative international dockers'organisation, a claim strenuously denied by all involved in the conference.

Nevertheless, the dockers and the international delegates who attended felt that this 'zonal conference' was a success in so far as it set out the next steps in the Liverpool dockers' international campaign. The conference culminated in the adoption of two resolutions. The first was concerned with the organisation of further financial and, most crucially, practical support for Liverpool from the international dock labour force. This included the call for a Day of Action on the 30 September 1996. This call went out to the ITF and its affiliates in order to demonstrate that the Liverpool dockers did not wish to be outside their organisation but did expect it to fulfil the promises of support that it had continually made throughout the dispute (see photostat 6a). One of the key points of this resolution concerned how to obtain solidarity from dockers in Germany and Belgium. It was decided the best solution was to send a delegation to both countries consisting of Liverpool dockers and international representatives from Sweden, Denmark and France. This, it was thought, would demonstrate, to dock workers and their unions in these countries, that the campaign was international and had secured practical support from other ports.

The second resolution concerned itself with the creation of an 'international dock workers alliance'. A Steering Committee was formed and a meeting planned for the weekend of the 25 October 1996 in France. (see photostat 6b).

It is clear, then, that 'internationalism' is central to the running of the dockers' dispute. But how has the 'international alliance' unfolded and what form has the campaign taken? Not suprisingly, the international strategy in many ways reflects the focus on the official trade union movement that has characterised this 'unofficial' dispute. At the first international conference the creation of the international body of dock workers was often referred to as a 'rank and file movement'. However this is not in fact the form that the 'alliance' has taken. The reasons for this are essentially to be found in the way in which the dockers have sought to create this support: it has been through approaches to trade union officials. These have ranged from local officials to trade union presidents, most notably John Bowers, President of the East Coast Longshoremen of America, and it is through these officials that they have contacted dockers or gained agreement to set picket lines. This is reflected in the status of those who have attended the international conferences: they are not rank and file dock workers as a rule, nor for the most part shop stewards, but in fact the equivalent of convenors, and local and national officials, clearly radical officials but officials nonetheless. The essence of the strategy has been to locate more 'left wing officials' within the internationl trade union bureaucracy, who can deliver some form of solidarity action from dock workers, rather than to create a layer of rank and file activists outside the union bureaucracies themselves. Of course there are differences between left-wing trade union leaders and right-wing leaders and the political difference between these two groups is important. However, both left and right wing officials have some things in common: their social position.[71] Trade union leaders, within Britain and overseas, exist as a conservative social stratum between capital and labour, whose purpose is to negotiate, albeit on behalf of workers, agreements between these two opposing social forces. This means they tend to vacillate between the demands of employers and workers, pushed first one way then another: expected by employers to be reasonable in 'difficult' negotiations and recognise the pressures placed on firms and employers by competition, and, on the other hand, expected to improve the work and living conditions of their members by obtaining concessions from employers.But trade union officials also have their own immediate interests to protect: higher than average wages; better working conditions; improved lifestyles and various beneficial work perks, for example. In these circumstances rank and file strategies, that is strategies that counterpose the strength  and organisational independence of the organised work force to the inertia of the trade union machinery, are a threat to all trade union leaders, whether they come from the right or the left. Rank and file strategies recognise the vascillating role of the bureaucracy. In the famous statement from the Clyde Workers' Committee:

We will support the officials just so long as they rightly represent the workers, but we will act independently immediately they mis-represent them....we claim to represent the true feelings of the workers...we can act immediately according to the merits of the case and the desire of the rank and file.[72]

Here the rank and file reserve the right to act independently of the union machinery if the workforce think they are acting in a way that is counter to their interests. The stewards in this dispute, however, have not adopted this strategy. This has led them to rely on the international 'left' trade union leaders but to ignore the fact that this layer can, and has, blocked activity and failed to deliver what they have promised. The most notable example being the promises by John Bowers that he could deliver the removal of the ACL whenever the dockers wished it (see chapter 4). It has also meant that a block has been placed on Liverpool dockers directly approaching other dock workers to support them. A good example of this is the position in Belgium. The support of the Belgian ports is seen by the stewards as crucial to the success of the European boycott and the fact that verbal and written promises of support have been received from Bob Baete have been seen as an important step forward. Yet the relationship between Bob Baete and the ITF has meant that these promises remain unfulfilled.

The strenuous denials, at the second international conference, that delegates were attempting to create a parallel organisation to the ITF is perhaps another clear demonstration of the stewards' position and that of their international colleagues. It would be wrong to suggest that there was not debate on this issue at the conference but the view that prevailed was that any dockers' organisation would need to operate in a way that would maintain the support of the ITF. This despite the fact that the ITF has repeatedly failed to turn their expressions of support into any tangible action and actively attempted to subvert the conference by telling Belgian and German delegates not to attend.

Nevertheless, this was again seen as a very positive conference in which further steps had been taken to secure their worldwide international campaign. It also emphasised the centrality of the international strategy in the campaign for reinstatement. Indeed it has now become the only strategy in terms of pursuing solidarity action from other workers.

In the week beginning 30 September 1996 a significant number of actions were taken against both ships and shipping lines operating out of Liverpool. These included strike action in Denmark, where dockers in four ports including Copenhagen and Aarhus, stopped work for the day. There was a complete boycott of ACL ships and containers in all ports in Sweden. In Australia there were go-slows, even though there were no ships from Liverpool in any of their ports. Meetings were held all over Spain to organise further activity. In Germany meetings were held for the first time. It was agreed to send financial support to the Liverpool dockers and to look at ways of organising secondary action, providing the ITF continued to support the dispute. On the 2 October in LeHavre dockers undertook a sixteen hour action against a vessel which has connections with CANMAR and CAST. In Montreal a rolling programme of work-to-rule action began on the port's freight liner service. This will affect 80% of the container traffic through-put in the docks and it was the Canadian dockers' intention to maintain this activity until CAST leave Liverpool or the dispute is resolved.

The creation of the international campaign, with no help from their own union and initially no funds, is a great achievement and should serve as a testament to the skills and hard work of the Liverpool dockers. It has brought the dockers both financial support and a level of 'practical' solidarity. The creation of the 'dockers alliance' is now seen as central to achieving the dockers' aim of a total blockade of Liverpool. However it has also been a difficult strategy to implement and the results have been uneven. Nevertheles, the stewards remain firmly committed to this strategy and view it as the key element to gaining their victory.

*Jimmy Davies and Jimmy Nolan with Jack Heyman of the West Coast of America's ILWU.*

*Tony Gardner, Billy Jenkins and Kevin Bilsborrow in Dublin, Ireland.*

*Jimmy Davies and Tony Nelson meet dockers in Montreal Canada.*

*The dockers display the banner used in the occupation of the gantries in Montreal. This was made for the dockers by the Montreal Longshoremen*

133

*Delegates at the first International Conference held in Liverpool Town Hall between the 17th and 23rd February 1996.*

*The Shop Stewards' Committee hosts the mass meeting at the end of the First International Conference, 23rd February 1996. Left to right, Terry Teague (standing), Bob Richie, Tony Melia, Terry Southers, Jimmy Davies Jnr, Mike Carden, Frank Lanigan, Jimmy Davies, Jimmy Nolan, Kevin Robinson, Bobby Morton and Tony Nelson. (Missing from photograph: Herbie Hollihead, Tony Russell, Andy Dwyer, Kevin Bilsborrow, Billy Jenkins)*

# Chapter 7

## Conclusion: The Struggle Goes On

At the time of writing, the Liverpool lock-out has just passed its first anniversary. The dockers have shown remarkable resilience, determination and courage: to fight against the odds for a year and more is testimony to their commitment to trade unionism, social justice and to a vision of the world where the rewards go to those who work and create society's wealth rather than to those who profit from the poverty and misery enshrined in existing work relationships. The dockers and the women of WOW rightly deserve admiration for the stand they have taken. But our aim is not to eulogise the dockers; it is to describe the events that produced the Liverpool lock-out and the campaign to end it. Our purpose in this final chapter is to take what may be termed a 'sober assessment': to look at what has occurred and what has been achieved and hence focus on the possibilities for the campaign as it enters its second year.

We start with a brief review of the causes of the dispute. As we argued in chapters one and two the present dispute has its roots in the abolition of the NDLS and MDHC's attempts to casualise dock work and hence cheapen their labour costs. MDHC tried several tactics in this regard: the attempt to incorporate the TGWU locally to police their members; the use of Torside as a 'wedge of casualisation'; and the imposition of new work contracts (in 1994) which put MDHC workers on 12 hour days. The consequences of these changes were dramatic affecting the health and well-being of dockers and their families. The resistance of the dockers to these tactics led MDHC to provoke a full confrontation with the workforce. As we argued, the evidence clearly indicates that the dispute was manufactured. One final piece of evidence supporting this thesis rests with the detail of MDHC's plans for the Liverpool docks complex. Over the last year MDHC has finalised their planning application to extend and redevelop the Liverpool port. Their aim is to turn Liverpool into a major 'hub' port - a major terminal capable of handling the largest of ships importing and exporting raw materials and goods for distribution to smaller ships, lorries and trains. As part of their plans they wish to close a number of roads around the docks, build a major rail terminal and establish and build a large roll-on, roll-off terminal at the Trafalgar docks within their port complex. The plans will have a major environmental and social impact on Liverpool. Success with this strategy will mean that MDHC will require fewer dockers, more casual working practices with people hired to meet short-term labour needs, and 'smooth operations' which means minimising dock-side disruptions. The existing unionised workforce represent a potential threat to MDHC's plans to put their profits before the lives of their workforce and those who live in the area around the docks. The dispute gave them the opportunity to get rid of problematic opponents.

Secondly, in response to the lock-out the Liverpool dockers have mounted a quite magnificent campaign for reinstatement. How should we assess it? The campaign has gone through a number of phases and encompassed a number of distinct strategies for victory. Strategies have developed out of the political debate that has taken place within the dispute and has been shaped by the dockers' own experiences, the influence of supporters among the wider political and trade union movement, the dominant political positions within the shop stewards' movement and the influence of the TGWU. Amongst these the most important factor shaping how the dispute has been run has been the activities and the political beliefs of the shop stewards. The shop stewards have been active on the docks for a considerable number of years, Jimmy Nolan for example, has been a shop steward since the late 1960's. Most of the present shop stewards' committee have been instrumental in re-establishing the union presence and shop steward representation in the post-abolition period, and have fought to offset the worst effects of casualisation embodied in the 1994 contracts. Not surprisingly, as a consequence, the stewards have won a great deal of respect from the workforce and have been the ones that the workforce has looked to provide the appropriate leadership during the dispute. However, the events of the last 20 years have also had an impact on the stewards. Many of the stewards believe that the last 20 years have taken a toll on the British working class movement and have an effect on what it is possible to achieve in any industrial dispute, and that industrial relations law has severely limited the capabilities of the labour and trade union movement. There is, of course, disagreement and debate amongst the stewards on these matters; they do not simply share the same political philosophies. Nevertheless, the ethos of 'collective responsibility' has meant that the stewards have presented a common front both to the dockers and to the supporters in the wider labour and trade union movement. It

137

means that political arguments and disagreements about the running of the dispute are aired at the daily stewards meetings, but are then suppressed to exhibit unity. In this sense we can identify a set of common beliefs or ideas that are presented by the shop stewards' committee - though they do not match exactly the political positions of all the stewards.

The dominant beliefs are: that the British working class is unable to deliver practical solidarity to the dockers, both as a result of the legal situation and the defeats workers have suffered at the hands of employers and governments over the last 20 years; that the TGWU is shackled by the law and unable to offer much open support; and thus it is necessary to look for alternative allies. These beliefs remain dominant within the leadership of the dispute despite the fact that there has been substantial solidarity from other workers produced by trade union and political activists from outside the docks. The regular levies at Sefton UNISON and AC Delco, the regular contributions from the shop stewards' committees at Fords, Vauxhall and British Aerospace and the vast sums donated by trade union branches up and down the country emphasise the level of support the dockers have and the willingness of workers to support the dockers' cause. The presence of Liverpool firefighters, Delco and Sefton UNISON workers, postal workers and engineers on the pickets, many bringing their banners to identify their union branch with the struggle, again identifies the possibilities. While the range and level of support the dockers received on the May Day Rally, with no backing from the official trade union movement, emphasised that activists outside the docks were willing to lead secondary action and, further, were able to mobilise the support of many of their members.

Yet despite these examples, the docks stewards have, for the most part, been unwilling to pursue this line of support. They believe that British workers will not support them in sufficient numbers, that secondary action breaks the law and that the combined effect of these will be to compromise the TGWU, which will have deleterious consequences on their relationship with the union and stop the 'unofficial' help they are obtaining. Thus they have avoided or, as the May Day events suggest, blocked the attempts to build secondary industrial action.

The stewards committee's beliefs have reinforced their strategy of looking for 'other supporters' outside the British trade union movement and, hence, the international tactic fits neatly with their perspective. The international strategy means that you do not have to ask for support from

138

the British working class, or break the law, nor compromise the TGWU: an international boycott will deliver the victory for Liverpool. At times it has seemed as if this tactic may deliver the victory the dockers desire. The removal of the ACL was clearly the high point of this campaign. But the international boycotts, go-slows and actions taken on ships using Liverpool have tended to be short-lived affairs: it is immensely difficult to maintain such actions over long periods of time. However, the international campaign could be easier to maintain if it were a supplement to an active blockade and campaign of secondary action within Britain - but this is a strategy most stewards have been unwilling to argue for.

The international focus also avoids direct confrontation with the TGWU. The relationship between the dockers and the TGWU has been tense during the dispute. The stewards and dockers clearly feel they should have received more support. The most obvious cause of disagreement has been the TGWU's refusal to regularly provide hardship payments and the stewards have been vocal in their criticism of the union in this regard. The stewards feel that they have had to badger the TGWU continually in order to receive any money from the union. The union has also failed to adequately publicise the dispute amongst its own members and has failed to offer active support to help build the various demonstrations, pickets and lobbies. They have also failed to support any form of secondary action, so TGWU members still work in the port and regularly cross pickets (a point MDHC raise in their own publicity about the dispute). However, the stewards are also in regular contact with Jack Adams and, through him, Bill Morris. Adams has been involved in all negotiations with MDHC, sometimes without any steward being present. On each occasion he has argued that he has obtained the best possible deal for the dockers though he has not obtained reinstatement. The dispute is run from Transport House with many of the costs of rooms, telephones and faxes borne by the union. The dispute is not official but the stewards do have a regular contact with, and an orientation to the union and its machinery. One of the stewards' concerns is to run the dispute in such a way that this relationship will not be seriously affected. The May Day events again emphasise the point. As Liverpool activists got organised and the strike call spread from local government and civil service workers and firefighters there was talk and discussion among the dockers of support for the growing idea of a 24-ß hour Liverpool general strike. At the time there was some disagreement among the stewards about what they could achieve (and many supported the call for a 24 hour stoppage), but the collective position was one that

139

moved away from calling for strike action and instead asked for attendance at the lunchtime rally. The reason was that the senior stewards did not want to ask for support (especially for illegal activities) over the union machinery. The result was a large demonstration with representatives from across the country and union banners from the breadth of the labour and trade union movement, but some dockers clearly felt it could have been better and that more could have been achieved.

The focus on international support has had a direct impact on many of the dockers involved in the dispute. A relatively small number of dockers have travelled abroad, another group of dockers has been involved in delegation work within Britain, together both represent a minority of the sacked dockers. A larger number are involved in daily and weekly pickets. But the activity of these dockers can also hide the fact that there has been a growing problem of 'inactivity'. From February the weekly mass meeting has included at least one demand from the stewards for more active participants, that the dockers should attend the pickets, go to the demonstrations or become involved in delegation work. However, in a sense this highlights a weakness in the dockers' strategy: if internationalism and the international dock labour force are going to win the dispute for Liverpool workers why do they need to attend 6 am pickets? Thus, the focus on the international strategy has also been a significant element in promoting inaction at home. It has also affected the weekly mass meetings. The mood of the meetings can swing sharply from week to week depending on what is occuring on the 'international front': a promise of a stoppage on a Liverpool bound ship or a success in the campaign against ACL or CAST produces an upbeat meeting, while the meeting can become restrained if international actions have not occurred or the prospects for action look slim.

Finally, as we argued in chapter 6, the international strategy itself is not, despite the claims, an international rank and file strategy. It is rather, a strategy that aims to bring on board left-wing, or 'progressive' sections of the international trade union bureacracy. It is similar to the various 'broad left' strategies that exist inside the trade union movement in Britain: it sacrifices the support of the rank and file of the union movement to the needs of left-leaning officials. In this dispute, one of the consequences, has been that, at crucial moments, the ITF have been in a position to undermine the international solidarity action that the dockers have been seeking to obtain.

The dockers and their families remain committed to the struggle for re-instatement. Their determined and principled stand deserves the full support of those who abhor the cruelty and deprivation of casual working practices and support the rights of workers to organise to defend their living standards and working conditions. It would be a tragedy if the dockers and their families were sacrificed by the trade union leaders for their adherence to a basic trade union principle of never crossing a picket line.

*The children asked if they could speak at the Anniversary Rally. Neil Fox represents their views when he said "our families will not give in; we have been through too much." 28th September 1996.*

141

*The Operational Services Division 'policing' the peaceful marchers on 28th September 1996.*

# Bibliography and Sources

## 1. Interviews and Mass Meetings

The majority of this book is based on taped interviews with participants in the present dispute and from our tapes of the weekly mass meetings and the international and national support conferences. When referring to interviewees we have often only used first names to maintain some anonymity, the 'downside' is that there are several participants with the same name! Quotations from or issues raised at mass meetings are referenced to the date the meeting occured. A complete set of our tapes will be held in the Department of Sociology, Social Policy and Social Work Studies, University of Liverpool. At the end of the dispute it is our intention to place a copy of the tapes with Liverpool City Libraries.

## 2. Dockers' information

Mersey Docks' Strike        Never Cross A Picket Line (Liverpool, 1996)
Committee,

Mersey Port Joint Shop   Submission on Behalf of Sacked Liverpool
Shop Stewards' Committee,   Dockworkers to the Employment Sub-Committee,
                            House of Commons, May 1996

Women of the                Stand By Our Men: The Story of the Women of the
Waterfront                  Waterfront (Liverpool, 1996)

## 3. Secondary Sources

M Allen,                    'Post-war Dock Strikes 1945-1955'
                            (North West Labour History Journal,
                            No. 15, 1990/91, pp. 82-96).

A Callinicos,  'The Rank-and-File Movement Today'
(International Socialism, Second Series,
No. 17, 1982 pp. 1-39).

T Cliff &  Marxism & Trade Union Struggle:
D Gluckstein,  The General Strike of 1926 (London, Bookmarks 1986).

S Davies,  'History in the Making:
The Liverpool Docks Dispute 1995-96'
(North West Labour History Journal, No 21, 1996/7).

B Hunter,  They Knew Why They Fought
(London, Index, 1994).

T Lane &  Strike at Pilkingtons (Suffolk, Fontana, 1971).
K Roberts,

J Pilger,  'The Forgotten Heroes'
(Guardian Weekend, 23 November 1996).

E Taplin,  The Dockers' Union. A Study of the National Union of
Dock Labourers 1889-1922
(Leicester University Press, 1985).

P Thompson,  The Voice of the Past
(New Edition, Oxford University Press, 1988).

D F Wilson,  Dockers: The Impact of Industrial Change
(Suffolk, Fontana, 1972).

NB See also material referred to in Notes pp 145-147.

# NOTES

1. See, for example, Innes, J. Thatcherism at Work Ch. 6, (OUP, 1987).
2. Editorial, Lloyd's List, 9.10.95.
3. See, for example, The (Liverpool) Daily Post, 26.2.96.
4. See the discussion in The Observer,15 September 1996 in the aftermath of the TUC Conference September 1996.
5. See, for example, Taplin, E., The Dockers' Union (Leicester University Press, 1985); Turnbull, P. & Wass, V. "The greatest game no more - Redundant dockers and the demise of dock work" (Work, Employment and Society, Vol. 8 No.4, 488-506); Turnbull, P., Woolfson, C., and Kelly, J., (Dock Strike: Conflict and Restructuring in Britain's Ports, Avebury, 1992); Wilson, D.F., Dockers (Fontana 1972); Hunter, B., They Knew Why They Fought (Index, 1994).
6. Wilson, *op cit.* pp.27-28.
7. Mayhew, H. Mayhew's London (1851, 1969 ed) London Spring Books.
8. Webb, B. My Apprenticeship (1887, 1971 ed) Penguin.
9. Rathbone, E. Inquiry into the Conditions of Labour at the Liverpool Docks (1904) Liverpool Economic and Statistical Society.
10. Wilson *op cit.* p.20.
11. *ibid.*
12. Allen, M. "Post-war dock strikes 1945-1955" North West Labour History Journal 15, 1990/91 p.82.
13. Hunter *op cit.* p.5.
14. Wherever appropriate we have used the oral testimonies of the present workforce and their families to describe, highlight and emphasise the points being made. When we submitted our first draft of the present text to the publisher's reviewers and some of our colleagues we were told by some that the dockers' memories and testimonies did not match the reality of aspects of working life on the docks in the 1950's and 1960's. We were told the 'pens' had gone, older workers (i.e. over 65's) did not work in the holds and that casualism had been abolished *de facto* because of the general shortage of labour in the post-war boom. We were directed to Wilson's excellent book to substantiate these claims. However, Wilson is much less clear cut and notes the existence of labour pens in Liverpool in the late 1960's and the number of older dockers still at work - claims which confirmed many of the dockers' accounts. This emphasises an important point: oral histories, testimonies and memories do need to be assessed against other sources and this applies as much to the memories of academics, often affected by their analysis of assumed changes to work practices over the last twenty years, as much as it does to those of participants being interviewed.
15. Allen *op cit.* p.82.
16. *ibid.* p.83.
17. Wilson *op cit.* p.94.
18. Allen *op cit.* p.83.

19. *ibid.* p.85.

20. *ibid.* p.83.

21. Hunter *op cit.* p.18.

22. See Hunter *ibid.*

23. *ibid.* p.135.

24. Turnbull & Wass *op cit.* p.493.

25. See Turnbull et al. *op cit.*

26. The Independent 8 April 1987 in Hunter *op cit.*

27. *ibid.*

28. *ibid.*

29. Hunter *op cit.*; Socialist Review June 1989.

30. Socialist Worker July 1989.

31. Hunter *op cit.* p.112.

32. Turnbull & Wass *op cit.*

33. Turnbull et al. *op cit.*

34. Merseyside Port Shop Stewards' Committee (1996) *Submission on Behalf of Sacked Liverpool Dockworkers to the Employment Sub-Committee*, House of Commons, May 1996, p.5.

35. *ibid.* p.13.

36. *ibid.* p.11.

37. *ibid.* p.12.

38. "Petition to Major" Dockers Charter No. 3, Jan. 1996.

39. WOW Stand By Our Men: The Story of the Women of the Waterfront (Liverpool) p.18.

40. See, for example, Liverpool Echo 26 Feb. 1996 and Daily Post 26 Feb. 1996.

41. "Dockers fight for all" Dockers Charter, No. 2 Dec. 1995.

42. See, for example, Lane, T & Roberts, K. Strike At Pilkingtons, (Fontana 1971).

43. Newsline 20 Feb. 1996.

44. Harvey, P. "Sacked dockers barred again" Liverpool Echo 10 Oct. 1995.

45. Roberts, N. "Dockers end strike only to find their jobs gone" Daily Post 6 Oct. 1995.

46. Harvey, P. "Dockers in police action warning" Liverpool Echo 6 Oct. 1995.

47. See, for example, Harvey, P. "Churches plea to docks chief" Liverpool Echo 11 Oct. 1995; Harvey, P. "MP's fury at bosses" Liverpool Echo 17 Oct. 1995; Hunt, A. "Dock bosses hit back at Labour" Liverpool Echo 2 Nov. 1995.

48. Leader, "Time for healing" Liverpool Echo 11 Oct. 1995.

49. Mersey Port Shop Stewards' Committee *op cit.* p.9.

50. *ibid.*

51. Liverpool Echo 6 Nov. 1995.

52. "London finally makes a flying start" Dockers Charter No.6 May 1996.

53. See, for example, the article: "Unity of all workers for a national support group committee" Dockers Charter No. 6 May 1996.

54. See, for example, Handley, M. "Bowing out" Daily Post 14 Nov. 1995; Harvey, P. "D-Day for docks" Liverpool Echo 15 Jan. 1996; Harvey, P. "Dock shares fall amid fears of ACL pull-out" Liverpool Echo 16 Jan. 1996; Harvey, P. "Deadline reprieve for dock company" Liverpool Echo 19 Jan. 1996; Harvey, P. "Dockers urge port boycott" Liverpool Echo 3 April 1996; Harvey, P. "Mersey Boycott Threat" Liverpool Echo 4 April 1996.

55. Liverpool Echo 11 April 1996.

56. Brauner, S. "Business Post" Liverpool Echo 21 Aug. 1996.

57. Harvey, P. "£87,000 pay rise for docks chief" Liverpool Echo 21 March 1996.

58. Harvey, P. "Iron curtain shields dock work from pickets" Liverpool Echo 30 Nov. 1995.

59. Harvey, P. "New Labour New Anger" Liverpool Echo 8 Oct. 1996.

60. Harvey, P. "Fired dockers wait on offer" Liverpool Echo 24 Jan. 1996; Doyle, M. "Mersey docks offers £7m to dockers" Daily Telegraph 26 Jan. 1996.

61. Mersey Port Shop Stewards' Committee *op cit.* p.10.

62. See, for example, Liverpool Echo 26 Feb. 1996; 1 May 1996.

63. Mersey Docks Strike Committee Never Cross A Picket Line (Liverpool 1996) p.18.

64. Newsline 20 Feb. 1996.

65. See, for example, Liverpool Echo 14 Dec. 1995 & 25 July 1996.

66. Harvey, P. "May Day rally in city centre" Liverpool Echo 1 May 1996.

67. This strategy is best summed up in various issues of the Dockers Charter. See, for example,"Dockers win worldwide backing" Dockers Charter No.2 Dec. 1995; "The World is our picket line" Dockers' Charter No. 3 Jan. 1996; "Globalization" Dockers Charter No.6 May 1996.

68. Mersey Port Strike Committee *op cit.* p.15.

69. *ibid.*

70. *ibid.* p.14.

71. See Cliff, T. & Gluckstein, D (1986) Marxism and Trade Union Struggle: The General Strike of 1926 (Bookmarks 1986).

72. Quoted in Callinicos, A. "The rank-and-file movement today" International Socialism (2nd Series, Vol. 17, 1982, p11).

*Solidarity on the Waterfront*

*Solidarity on the Waterfront*

*Solidarity on the Waterfront*